THE COMING GREAT CHURCH

THE MACMILLAN COMPANY
NEW YORK · BOSTON · CHICAGO
DALLAS · ATLANTA · SAN FRANCISCO

MACMILLAN AND CO., LIMITED
LONDON · BOMBAY · CALCUTTA
MADRAS · MELBOURNE

THE MACMILLAN COMPANY
OF CANADA, LIMITED
TORONTO

THE
Coming Great Church

ESSAYS ON CHURCH UNITY

Theodore O. Wedel, PH.D., S.T.D.

Warden of the College of Preachers
and
Canon of Washington Cathedral

New York

THE MACMILLAN COMPANY

1945

First Printing

A WARTIME BOOK

PRINTED IN THE UNITED STATES OF AMERICA
BY THE VAIL-BALLOU PRESS, INC., BINGHAMTON, N. Y.

FOREWORD

The substance of this book was originally in the form of lectures delivered at the Philadelphia Divinity School (Episcopal) under the John Bohlen Lectureship. The trust provides that "the subject of such lectures shall be such as is within the terms set forth in the will of the Reverend John Bampton, for the delivery of what are known as the Bampton Lectures at Oxford, or any other subject distinctively connected with or relating to the Christian religion." I thank trustees and patient listeners.

Excerpts from three chapters of the book have been published in *Religion in Life*, *Theology Today*, and *Christendom*. I gratefully acknowledge permission to reprint the portions incorporated in the expanded version of the book.

Grave omissions in this book will be readily noted. A study of the doctrine of the Church might be expected to draw heavily upon Eastern Orthodox thought. Rich insights on the Church await disclosure and interpretation as western and eastern Christendom create friendship across centuries of alienation—as, indeed, they are beginning to do in the ecumenical movement. But in dealing with the theology of the Eastern Orthodox Churches, Pope's warning applies: "A little learning is a dangerous thing." In this field my learning is little, indeed, and it seemed best to limit the scene of my discussion to our western Christian culture, in which the great controversies on the problem of the Church are more familiar to us. It ought, however, soon to be impossible to ignore the contribution which Eastern Orthodox thought can make to a recovery of a view of the Church which clearly has preserved some of the forgotten characteristics of the classic centuries of Church life which we, through much tribulation, are trying to rediscover in the West.

Another omission, more serious perhaps, is my failure to allude more than cursorily to the several notable experiments already made, or in prospect, in actual Church unification. The United Church of Canada here comes to mind, as also the South India Union Scheme—the latter, though still under debate, bridging even the Catholic-Protestant chasm by a union of Anglicans, Methodists, and Congregationalists. A third important reunion project is under negotiation now between the Presbyterian Church in the U.S.A. and the Protestant Episcopal Church. Wrestling with concrete problems of Church unity, as I have myself been privileged to do as participant in the Presbyterian-Episcopalian negotiations, sharpens underlying issues. It is the urge to clarify, for myself at least, some of these basic considerations of the *doctrine* of the Church that has led to this series of lectures. I have, accordingly, not attempted to discuss actual projects of unification, since these enter areas of ecclesiastical statesmanship which require special treatment.

The ambiguity of the word "Catholic" can be the despair of any writer on the doctrine of the Church. Historically and controversially "Catholic" and "Protestant" (or "Evangelical") stand over against each other. But dig below the surface of this contrast in history, and the outline of the word "Catholic" soon becomes blurred. A Protestant reciting the Christian creeds may believe in the Catholic Church as much as any Romanist. Evangelical Christianity has preserved vital elements of catholicity of which Rome scarcely dreams. Indeed, the united evangelical Church of the future may be more "catholic," as this concept is part of basic Christian Faith, than any catholicism which has as yet appeared in history. Nevertheless, the confusion in the use of the word remains. I have tried to keep alive some distinctions in its use, but have not avoided all ambiguity. The context in which the word appears must be trusted to make the meaning partly clear.

If I am right in the conviction voiced in this book that the doctrine of the Church, with the related doctrine of the Holy Spirit, are the forgotten doctrines of Christian tradition, even immature and tentative explorations have their value. My own suggestions looking toward the solving of problems may soon be corrected or superseded. I have at times, I fear, expressed them more provocatively than fully balanced truth warrants. I take comfort in a saying of Bishop Mandell Creighton: "The two chief means of teaching are exaggeration and paradox. One or the other is needed to attract attention and show reason for independent thought." My aim would be fulfilled if this book could contribute toward the awakening of greater concern for Church unity and the willingness to listen to what, in our day of the Lord, "the Spirit saith to the churches."

THEODORE O. WEDEL

CONTENTS

THE COMING GREAT CHURCH

INTRODUCTION

A whimsical psychologist once propounded the question how a fish would describe water. He came to the conclusion that a fish (even a talking fish) would not be able to describe water. A fish lives in water. A fish knows nothing else. Water, for a fish, is something taken for granted.

A somewhat similar inhibition has beset Christian thought in regard to the Church. All Christian experience is, in a sense, ecclesiastical experience. John Calvin (of whom many might not expect such words) calls the Church our "mother" and speaks of "how useful and even necessary it is for us to know her; since there is no other way of entrance into life, unless we are conceived by her, born of her, nourished at her breast, and continually preserved under her care." [1] Yet precisely because the Church is "mother," she has, like human motherhood, far too often been taken for granted. Theologians have had comparatively little to say about her. We usually think, for example, of the Middle Ages as the great "Church" centuries of history. But it is in its doctrine of the Church that mediaeval theology is at its weakest. You will look in vain in the *Summa Theologica* of St. Thomas Aquinas for more than a cursory treatment of the Church. Even in our day the doctrine of the Church has as yet not come fully into its own. No ecumenical conference on Faith and Order has thus far wrestled directly with it, nor given it full honor on its agenda.

The doctrine of the Church, in fact, may turn out to be

[1] *Institutes* 4.1.4.

I

the great rediscovery of our day of Christian history. It has slumbered long in the subconscious of Christian Faith. The hundreds of schisms which have rent the Body of Christ were mostly caused by battles on other doctrinal issues. We were content to leave the doctrine of the Church alone. For this might have meant the emergence of a bad conscience in the midst of our blithe denominational divorcings.

But, thanks to God's judgments, we have entered a new age. A bad conscience has at last been vouchsafed us. We are learning to sing a modern hymn like

> In Christ there is no East or West,
> In him no South or North,
> But one great fellowship of love
> Throughout the whole wide earth.

And while we readily apply this generous sentiment to the varied heathen in distant lands whom our missionaries are baptizing into our particular denominational Church, it will gradually dawn on us that it applies even more to the rival Church neighbor on our own street. Ecclesiastical isolationism, like that of nations, is surely doomed.

Yet, as in the days of Amos, the day of the Lord may be, first of all, a day of darkness and not light (Amos 5:18). Judgment is upon us. Have we of the divided Christian flock become even dimly aware as yet of what is happening to us? We are the people of God. We are the Fellowship of the Holy Spirit. Our most sacred rite is that of Holy Communion. We still hear the command of the Church's Founder: "Do this in remembrance of me." But do we? The terrifying fact is that we do not. We are separated at the holy table. Hence God permits rival fellowships to come to birth. He raises children of Abraham from stones. If Christians cannot exhibit brotherhood, secular "Churches" spring up which witness to fellowship, even if only on the natural plane of economic need. The very word Communion is being taken from us. The disciples of Karl Marx also use it now, and are finding in it the secret of their rebirth into a new life of corporate solidarity. Communists have almost more right than Christians to apply to themselves the verse of the New Testament (Gal. 3:28): "There is neither Jew nor Greek, there is neither bond nor free, there is neither male nor female: for ye are all one. . . ."

The doctrine of the Church—as indeed the Church herself—can be taken for granted by Christians no longer. The rival secular "Churches" of our age will fulfill our neglected function of creating brotherhood if we do not. Have we not forgotten the first law of the Communion of the Holy Spirit—"that ye love one another"? Has our individualism brought us to the dreadful pass that God must bring summary judgment upon a second chosen people as He once did upon a first? We may well listen to the words of St. Paul, addressed to the Israel of his century: "It was necessary that the word of God should first have been spoken to you: but seeing ye put it from you, and judge yourselves unworthy of everlasting life, lo, we turn to the Gentiles" (Acts 13:46). For Gentiles, read Communists, or even the pitiful folk who groped for communion and brotherhood under a Hitler, and this verse can assume ominous significance.

To rediscover the full meaning of the Church will not be easy for modern Christians. We are a people of God "scattered and peeled" (Isaiah 18:2). Ecumenical theology is surely only in its infancy. The very phrase still sounds novel in our ears, though the onsweep of movements toward Church unity will probably make us familiar with it. Reunion will be endlessly costly. None of us as yet fully want it despite generous lip-service to ecumenical ideals. We want it on our terms, with *our* Church still occupying the chief seats at the coming reunion feast.

The following essays will be found to be guilty also of the sin of Church parochialism. I write as a minister in the "Protestant Episcopal Church in the United States of America" —one of the churches, now spread over the world, subsumed under the more general title of "Anglican." To many outside my Communion my observations on the problem of Church reunion will seem woefully lacking in understanding of other traditions. To many within my Communion they will, in turn, appear to have sacrificed on the altar of premature ecumenicity some of the most sacred of Anglican convictions. But I must perforce start from where I am.

To make clear at the outset what prejudices may be expected in this book I venture upon a few paragraphs of autobiography. My ecclesiastical experiences have not been unique. But they do lay claim to acquaintance with at least two Church traditions. Like hundreds of those who serve in the Anglican ministry today (particularly in America), I was not born an Episcopalian. Some of my more indigenous Anglican brethren may perhaps trace some heterodoxies to this cause.

My ancestral Church is that of the Mennonites. I was born in a Mennonite parsonage, on a college campus in a midwestern, typically American, town. There exist in America a dozen or more separate Mennonite "Churches." Ours was a branch which came originally from Holland and had retained many Dutch customs. Unlike the more publicized Mennonites of Pennsylvania, it practiced no ascetic distinction of dress and custom. We mingled freely with American neighbors and were almost too easily Americanized. But as a Church our community was still vigilantly separatist—an analogue on Protestant soil of a Catholic "religious" order, as is the sect-type of Church life generally.

As I look back upon the experiences of youth, I must admit that my ancestral communion could boast of a quality of Christian social living which I have not seen equalled anywhere since. Corporate brotherhood approached New Testament patterns. A divorce or a dispute involving a civil law court was simply unheard of. Charity and missionary giving were more than generous. Church government was by a group of "elders." All elders could preach, but only one (usually called "chief elder," though sometimes "bishop") could preside at the holy table. It was a Church order which reduplicated what might have been found in many an early Christian congregation. This evangelical primitivism was a mark of Church life throughout.

The Holy Communion, for example, was an awesome corporate rite. St. Paul's warnings (I Cor. 11) about unworthy partaking were taken literally. The Holy Supper was celebrated only some four times a year, but preparations extended over weeks. Those with burdened conscience, or those who had offended the community, were dealt with by the Session of elders by way of confession and corporate absolution. On a Sunday before the Communion, announcement was made to the congregation of the Session's absolvings, with the command: "Gossip on these matters is to stop from this day forward." And it did!

At the youthful age of eighteen I became organist in the little Episcopal Church in our community. My conversion to Anglicanism was almost immediate and complete, and I was shortly confirmed, though another twenty years passed before I entered the ministry. A sharper contrast in ecclesiastical traditions can hardly be imagined, and I have puzzled

since how to explain such a sudden transfer of loyalties.
Certain it is, if one may judge one's own past, that my entrance into a relatively more "Catholic" form of Church life
saved me from some of the dangers surrounding my dis-
turbed generation. College and university years followed,
and a decade of "Liberalism" and half-agnosticism. Yet the
tie with the Episcopal Church somehow held, as the ties
with an evangelical background might not have held. The
Church's liturgy could never be forgotten. It was always
there in memory as a subconscious arouser of conscience.
The Church's historic traditions could not be ignored, nor
undermined by cheap scepticism. Membership in a local
Christian flock could have been escaped, but not membership in the Church of history, marks of which even the small-
est Anglican chapel still bears. I can understand why a Romanist finds it almost impossible to break completely with
his Church, while for many a Protestant such a break is often
comparatively easy.

It has taken many years, indeed, before I have come to
recognize again the full value of the evangelical heritage
with which my life in the Church began. I see that value now
—and the rediscovery has led me to appreciate once more
Reformation evangelicalism generally. I hope the following
pages will give some evidence of this appreciation. But my
experience leads me to a criticism of Protestant evangelical
Church life also.

The trouble with evangelicalism is that it demands too
much too soon. Most of us are simply not ready for it. I
know that I was not ready for it in my youth. Or, to put it
in another way, modern evangelicalism is a plant growing
in too shallow a soil. It tries to achieve sanctification by way
of short cuts. In earlier eras, when the mediaeval inheritance
of institutional Christianity was still in our blood, when the

Bible was still uncritically accepted, when secular life was still suffused with Christian conscience, this weakness of Protestant evangelicalism was not fully apparent. But can any observer fail to see that weakness today? Is it not yielding on many fronts to humanist Liberalism? Evangelicalism enshrines values, nevertheless, which are the heart of true Catholicism. These should be Catholicism's goal. To achieve the freedom of the Christian man which Luther rediscovered, or the maturity of Christian conviction evidenced at a traditional Methodist class meeting, or the power of a corporate Holy Supper—who would fail to recognize these as high-water marks of Christian experience? Many a Catholic could look upon them with envy. The Liturgical Movement within Rome is groping for some of these achievements of Protestant evangelicalism in ways which seem to a Protestant belated and sometimes almost pitiful.

Evangelical Christianity is, in some essentials of Christian conviction and life, an unquestioned advance over Catholicism. It came later in history, and it may have needed the Middle Ages to produce it. The problem is how to preserve it or to reproduce it in an age when the long disciplines of mediaeval Catholicism have been forgotten. Can you produce it without previous tutoring—in liturgical worship, in institutional loyalties, in sacramental certainties? Evangelical Church life is a kind of ecclesiastical primitivism. It is modelled consciously upon New Testament analogues. Yet any student of culture can testify that conscious primitivism is not really primitive. The Christian Church is an historical, not a legal or ideological fact. Evangelical Church life ignores history—even its own history.

Roman Catholic Church life appears to a Protestant as mechanical and legalistic. At its worst, it looks half-pagan. And so perhaps it is, though the ancient paganism which lurks in the Catholic tradition is, in comparison with modern godlessness, "high" religion. Institutionalism in the Roman Church, let us grant, is divinized and partially substituted for the Gospel. A means is transformed into an end. I shall criticize Catholicism freely in the following chapters. But it is for lack of Catholic elements that evangelical Christianity is weak today.

Take legalism as an example. There is no doubt that legalism is one of the dangers in Christian life. But even St. Paul grants it the function of "schoolmaster to bring us to Christ" (Gal. 3:24). Catholic legalism still partly fulfills this task. Obedience to the "dominical precept"—attendance at Mass every Lord's Day—may seem to the Protestant a poor substitute for full congregational communion. But at least it brings the Catholic to his Church and even to a "breaking of bread," if only at the priest's altar. It maintains his consciousness of belonging to the people of God. Has the Protestant a fit substitute? Legalism is a mark of evangelical Church life also. But it often takes the form of the Puritan taboo, a legalism of sanctification. A good deal can be said for Puritan taboos. They once were symbols of belonging to a corporate society, separated from the world. But does not such legalism, divorced from its social anchorage, begin at the wrong end of Christian experience? Should enthusiasm for Prohibition or some other asceticism be the *first* mark of Church membership? Might this mark not still be the obeying of the ancient command, "Gather me this people together, and I will make them hear my words"? (Deut. 4:10).

Protestant freedom—free worship, free prayer, release from priestly bondage, lay participation in councils, self-government of congregations—are precious achievements of Reformed Christianity. Institutionalism, however, can be disdained to the point where the individual Christian or the independent flock are left naked and alone. The freedom of individualistic evangelicalism needs corporate protection once more. It cries aloud for institutional safeguards. It is tempting (to use an analogy) to idealize the love of husband and wife to where it will flourish regardless of outward props. But most families need a house and a home and the ritual of settled routine. Christians need each other, and they need the communal home of an institutional Church. They need the witness of historic tradition; they need outward and visible sacraments. They need an ecumenical Church order.

John Foster, a Methodist missionary to China, whose book *Then and Now* I shall quote more than once in the following pages, writes: "A Congregationalist missionary in India complained to me that something was going far wrong with one of the neighboring churches. 'In the old days I, as senior missionary, would have stepped in and put it right. But now, with the progress of devolution, it is another, and an Indian minister's pastorate. We ought to have some central authority. . . .' 'A bishop?' said I. 'You don't seem to me to be talking Congregationalism.' 'Congregationalism?' he replied. '*They are not up to that yet.*' " [2]

A sentence of Rudolf Sohm has become famous and is often quoted: "The natural man is a born Catholic." The epigram is usually employed as an indictment of Catholicism. No doubt it can thus be rightly used to define the compromise with the Pelagian relaxing of conscience which characterizes much of Catholic legalism. But might not the evangelical churchman, granted that he can, at his best, boast of an ethically loftier tradition, examine this epigram afresh? Perhaps Catholicism has something to teach us. We

[2] John Foster, *Then and Now*, Student Christian Movement Press, 1942, page 53.

all *begin* as "natural man." Evangelical freedom is a difficult achievement. It may call for precisely a Catholic institutionalism as a base. Evangelical Christianity may need to rebuild its foundations.

My experience, as the preceding paragraphs show, seem to have led me far from the evangelical Church of my youth. And yet not so far either. The wheel comes full circle. For unless the ecumenical Catholic Church of the future can retain evangelicalism at its center, it will sin against the Holy Ghost. It is for the sake of the precious jewel of evangelical Faith and social witness to the Gospel that any Catholicism should exist.

I have no doubt yielded, in the following pages, to the temptation of idealizing my own Church. Somehow, I cannot help myself. For Anglicanism, at its best, has tried to combine a Catholic foundation of Church order and liturgical solidity with evangelical Faith and congregational brotherhood. Yet how easily either of these emphases are absolutized and made to rule over the other! Anglicanism, too, needs to emerge from its isolation and become part of a larger whole. Only the ecumenical Great Church can produce the full fruit of the Holy Spirit.

One striking example of the need of a truly ecumenical corporateness (which Anglicanism is not) to solve our Church problems lies in the area of discipline already discussed. Anglicanism, along with the other Reformation churches, has visibly failed in this. Anglo-Catholics are tempted to solve the problem by reintroducing the alluring disciplines of Rome. One may express grave doubt that this solution will serve. We may, indeed, look to Rome for a stimulation of Church conscience. But Rome did not achieve her disciplines by a *tour de force*, or by arbitrary legislation.

Her unifying disciplines, right or wrong, are an almost un-
conscious result of her massive historic corporate existence.
She still gives to her children the sense of "belonging" to a
Great Assembly, a Catholic Church. And "belonging" implies common customs and symbols—if nothing more than
not eating meat on Fridays. But mere imitation of Rome's
disciplines will not create another Catholic Church. It may
merely create another perfectionist sect. The road to Church
discipline is that of recreating corporateness. The ecumenical Church, when reborn, will recreate disciplines and much
else of wonder in the sight of men and of God.

Is there, in truth, a hope for the preservation of evangelical
Protestantism except by way of recovery of the Great
Church? In earlier generations of anchored social living the
separatist sect, or the larger denomination, could give to its
members the strength of corporate "belonging." Each could
be a little Catholicism. But that day is over. Modern nomad-
ism has torn us from our moorings. We are, most of us,
lonely and weak individualist Christians, lost in the giant
impersonal monopolies of economic and political imperial-
isms. We hunger, not merely for the Faith of our fathers,
but for fellowship in that Faith. We hunger for brotherhood. We hunger for personal relationships. The Church has
all these gifts. Where else shall we find them?

For the secular brotherhoods which are arising today in
judgment upon the divided people of God are ultimately
going to prove delusions. They cannot offer what they
promise. "Assyria, the rod of mine anger," said Isaiah as he
witnessed God's tool of judgment threatening his people.
But the Assyrians did not become the chosen people.

The flaw in all secular brotherliness, in contrast to brotherhood in Christ, is that it has no Cross, no atonement, no

forgiveness of sins. It is ultimately cruel. It must wield the
sword. Some form of socialism may well be the necessary
economic and political system of the future. But it will perish soon unless it has the Church of God in its midst, if only
as a saving remnant. Take eternity out of time and the sense
of human brotherhood is at first heightened. There are no
eternal arms beyond the cold stars. We have only each other,

> with dependence placed
> On the human heart's resource alone,
> In brotherhood bonded close and graced.[3]

But if help in our journey through the blind tragedy of time
comes from human love alone, how create that love? Will
economic need suffice, or the fellowship of race or class?
And if so, will it not be a fellowship of hate as well as love?
Sin *within* the human heart, in a purely secular world, becomes a meaningless concept. The struggle between good
and evil becomes *class*-warfare. Temporal society must right
every wrong here and now. There is no Lamb of God taking
away the sins of the world, no Church for "sinners."

> Arise, you prisoners of starvation!
>   Arise, you wretched of the earth,
> For justice thunders condemnation,
>   A better world's in birth.
> No more tradition's chains shall bind us,
>   Arise, you slaves; no more in thrall!
> The earth shall rise on new foundations,
>   We have been naught, we shall be all.
>
> Toilers from shops and fields united,
>   The union we of all who work;
> The earth belongs to us, the workers,
>   No room here for those who shirk.

[3] Thomas Hardy, *A Plaint to Man.*

How many on our flesh have fattened!
But if the noisome birds of prey
Shall vanish from the sky some morning
The blessed sunlight still will stay.

The *Internationale* is sung in our day by millions of men. It is the *Te Deum* of a new religion. It is a strange compound of love and hate, of judgment and apocalyptic hope. It smells of the sweat and the grime of factory town and city slum. It symbolizes the hunger of subdued generations for bread and a place in the sun, and, above all, for fellowship. It reminds readers of the New Testament of allusions to sheep who have not been fed. It is not pleasant reading.

Yet those of us who are still Christians in the midst of the social turmoil of our time had better read it and ponder its meaning. For this, in all likelihood, is the kind of a world in which the Christian Church will have to live. Class warfare has not touched our western democracies as yet, and let us hope that it can be averted. Secular godlessness may be held at bay. The coming of secular justice itself may forestall revolution. Remnants of Christian conscience may restrain the will to power of our nascent Fascist or Communist minorities. But the success, in recent generations, of weaving either extreme of our social class structure into *our* Christian brotherhood has not been conspicuous.

Eventually it is we, the people of God, who will have to recreate out of our warring multitudes the true brotherhood of repentance and forgiveness under the Cross of Christ. This brotherhood is not of class or economic need, or even of frail human love. It is the mighty act of a living God. Shall we be given time? Perhaps, if we of the Christian Church rediscover brotherhood ourselves. The dispersed Fellowship of the Holy Spirit must come to corporate self-consciousness again. We must reunite as the one Family of God.

As this Family, scattered over all parts of the globe and divided into quarrelling households, reassembles on God's holy mount, forgotten prophecies may be fulfilled and we shall see the glory of the Lord revealed. "Thus saith the Lord, I will even gather you from the peoples, and assemble you out of the countries where ye have been scattered. I will surely assemble, O Jacob, all of thee; I will surely gather the remnant of Israel; I will put them together as the sheep of Bozrah, as the flock in the midst of their pasture; they shall make great noise by reason of the multitude of men. At that time I will bring you again, even in the time that I gather you: for I will make you a name and a praise among all people of the earth, when I turn back your captivity before your eyes, saith the Lord" (Ezekiel 11:17; Micah 2:12; Zephaniah 3:20).

I

THE COMING GREAT CHURCH

In December of the year 1938 there met, at Madras, India, a conference of the International Missionary Council. This, with the exception of the World Conference of Christian Youth the following summer, was the last world gathering of Christians before the outbreak of the Second World War —the last in a generation which had seen a whole series of similar ecumenical conferences. The thunder clouds of global conflict were on the horizon. China and Japan had already seized the sword. Looking prophetically across the flaming ramparts of the spreading tragedy, the conference issued this call:

"In all humility and penitence we are constrained to declare to a baffled and needy world that the Christian Church, under God, is its greatest hope. The decade since last we met has witnessed an increasing unification of the body of Christ. As we meet here from over sixty nations out of every continent, we have discovered afresh that unity is not merely an inspiration but a fact. . . . Our nations are at war with one another; but we know ourselves brethren in the community of Christ's Church. Our peoples increase in suspicion and fear of one another; but we are learning to trust each other more deeply through common devotion to the one Lord of us all. Our governments build instruments of mutual destruction; we join in united action for the reconciliation of humanity. Thus in broken and imperfect fashion the

15

Church is even now fulfilling its calling to be within itself a foretaste of the redeemed family of God which He has purposed humanity to be. . . . By faith, but in deep assurance, we declare that this body which God has fashioned through Christ cannot be destroyed." [1]

A Methodist missionary present at this conference commented on it as follows:

"As we gathered at Madras, representatives of Christ's Church from every land under the sun, some of us thought we heard our Lord saying, 'Blessed are the eyes which see the things that ye see: for I say unto you, that many prophets and kings desired to see the things which ye see and saw them not' (Luke 10:23). Yes, indeed, was ever a generation like ours? The universal nature of the Church, true as an ideal from the time of our Lord and His Apostles, we saw as no Christians in nineteen centuries have seen, worthily represented in the actual and the concrete. This also has happened in our lifetime. God is not mocked. The world is not left at the mercy of a madman. Present in God's world, and never so widely established is God's Church, the central point of His working, the instrument for the fulfillment of His purposes, already in itself 'a foretaste of the redeemed family of God which He has purposed humanity to be.' The City of God remaineth. Lift up your hearts!" [2]

These are words, we may admit, of an enthusiast, thrilled as only a missionary can be, perhaps, over the miracle of geographical catholicity in our time. The Great Church is here—in space. The Gospel has penetrated the farthest corners of our world just ahead of the aeroplane—a fact which may turn out to be a major event in world history.

[1] *The World Mission of the Church*, page 19; *The Authority of the Faith*, Madras Series, Vol. I, pages 192 f.

[2] John Foster, *Then and Now*, Student Christian Movement Press, 1942, pages 39–40.

And this spread of Christianity has happened in our time. Professor Latourette, in his monumental history of Christian Missions, can devote three of seven volumes to the nineteenth century. It is this period of Christian expansion which he calls the "Great Century," in comparison even with the age of St. Paul.[3]

The Great Church already here? Yes, in one sense. No Christian using the word "Church" from henceforth can wholly ignore the meaning which it can bear as describing a world-embracing community of believers in Christ as Lord. The commandment, "Go ye into all the world," has been met. This far-flung community is awaking to self-consciousness. It is rediscovering itself as a mysterious act of God in history, the bearer of yet scarcely tested powers. The twentieth century is recapitulating the age of the apostles. Historians of missions speak commonly of the Older and the Younger Churches. The Younger Churches are closer in outlook to the first century than to the sixteenth or even eighteenth. What does the age of religious wars or of Catholic-Protestant persecutions mean to them? They can understand, on the basis of the miracle of their own creation, the epistles of St. Paul. They can scarcely understand the literature of Christian schisms which still fashions the thinking of the older Church groups.

Hence it is that from these Younger Churches comes a special cry to their Mother Churches for unity. Geographically the Christian body of believers may be catholic in the sense of external dispersion over our globe. But internally it is not catholic. It is not the Great Church. "By schisms rent asunder," yet by definition both one and holy, it testifies against its own message. We who live in the older regions of

[3] K. S. Latourette, *A History of the Expansion of Christianity*, 7 vols., Harper, 1937.

Christendom do not feel this tragic paradox as does the Church on the mission field. We are accustomed to seeing our twelve or more denominational Church spires in every town, each proclaiming its own version of the Faith. Familiarity has robbed the sin of disunion of its shame. Yet the fact remains that "a divided Church belies its own Creed. It warns the world against its own Gospel. Our thought still moves in a fatally false atmosphere. We have come to regard as normal and inevitable that against which about half of the New Testament is a passionate and sustained appeal." [4]

Has the sin of disunion driven any of us to full repentance? Or any Church? One may well doubt it. No Church with creed or confession still even vaguely in the historic Christian tradition denies belief in One Church. Yet how easily is disunity rationalized. Rome denies responsibility for it. She may acknowledge blunders and the sins of individual popes and clergy, but the sin of schism itself she lays on the shoulders of those whom she excommunicates. Massive guardian of the centuries, she is convinced that the march of Christians toward unity will sooner or later reach the walls of her fortress. And she hopes to win an easy victory. She tempts to capitulation. Let the forces of disunity run their course—the swifter they run the sooner, she predicts, they will run her way. Probably no Christian institution in the world today looks into the future with less fear. This equanimity of proud aloofness may be her undoing. I certainly see no hope, for the present, in the prospect of Rome's repentance. But of her more will be said later.

Leaving Rome aside, and limiting our view to the Churches which in our western Christendom have broken away from Rome, the outlook for unity seems at first hopeless enough.

[4] F. R. Barry, in *The Guardian*, June 28, 1929.

Enthusiasts for the ecumenical movements of our generation can present impressive arguments for optimism, and I
would not want to belittle these. My argument will be
optimistic also. Yet ecumenical experiments and conferences, however useful in their way, will have to depend for
their effectiveness upon winning the support of the Churches
themselves. In the Protestant sections of Christendom atom-
ism has become an entrenched tradition. In a gloomy mood
P. T. Forsyth, himself a convinced Protestant, once asked
the fateful question: "Is nothing to remain of Protestantism
at last but the credit of having shaken hierarchy and of having
referred religion to an inner but atomic experience of some
feeble sort?" [5] The very words "Church" and "Churchman"
have, for many Protestants, lost all theological meaning.
They do not connote a mighty act of God, nor a membership in a massive corporate mystery, of which the massive-
ness of Rome itself is only a faint token.

I shall not, however, dwell now upon the obvious fact
that Protestant Christianity is, on its institutional side, the
Church in fragments. An observer from the Catholic half of
Christendom may find some excuse for predicting the even-
tual dissolution of Protestantism. What chance, so the Catholic would argue, has Protestantism in the coming era when
it must confront institutional rivals of gigantic powers? The
day of Protestant individualism is over. Secularism was once,
too, individualistic and atomized. Protestant reliance upon
Bible and individual conscience could, accordingly, maintain itself for a few centuries. It could still live on inherited
capital, carried over from its Catholic past. It was and is in
Catholic eyes a parasite upon Catholic tradition. But our

[5] P. T. Forsyth, *The Church and the Sacraments*, Hodder & Stoughton,
1912, page 103.

world is atomized no longer. Secularism is itself becoming corporate. Only Catholic Christianity can hope to maintain itself.

This Catholic argument has, indeed, great force. Well may Protestantism heed it. We shall have to deal more fully later with the clashing of Catholic-Protestant views of the Church. May it suffice here to indicate, however, that the Catholic prophecy of coming victory may be a little premature. Let the Catholic observer observe again and more deeply. He may see, if he is wise, strange stirrings in that belittled Protestant world.

For Protestantism is beginning to speak again of the Great Church, the Catholic Church of Christian Creed and Christian Faith. If the age of individualism is truly receding in contemporary history, Protestant leadership is aware of this momentous fact. Contemporary history is forcing this fact upon our attention in unmistakable events. The Protestant Churches—and here the Catholic is surely right—will have to turn about and become "Catholic" or perish. The Protestant era, as such, may be over and a post-Protestant era emerging. And this new age will have to be "Catholic." The Church as a corporate, historical, social fact will have to be rediscovered. Such a rediscovery may, however, not be quite so difficult as an observer from the outside imagines. The Reformation tradition knows some things about the Church of which historic Catholicism itself is ignorant. The Reformation was a revolt against an authoritarian and tyrannical Church order. It was not a revolt against the doctrine of the Church. For a time at least a true people-Church appeared in history—a rediscovery of the *ecclesia* of the New Testament. I write as an Anglican and cannot escape the conviction that in Anglicanism one such people-Church, retaining a Catholic Church order, yet remaining evangelical, became partially realized. Anglicanism has lived for four hundred years by its Book of Common Prayer. The very title indicates a break with mediaeval tradition and yet a retention of a Catholic idea of the Church. I cannot escape, therefore, the further conviction that the Great Church, as it reëmerges in Protestant Christendom, will find in the Anglican tradition an invaluable guide.

Nothing in Reformation doctrine prevents the Reformation churches from rediscovering the vision of the Great Church. I would agree with P. T. Forsyth, who writes as a Congregationalist, when he says, "The Reformation certainly made religion personal, but it did not make it individualist." [6]

Nevertheless, it is true that for centuries the idea of the Great Church has been lost or minimized in the Protestant world. Subjective individualism has ruled in the place of loyalty to a corporate Church. How this loss of catholicity came about is a complex story. The Reformation was succeeded, or even accompanied, by the Renaissance and soon surrendered much to the latter. The two movements have been intertwined ever since. And the Renaissance knew little about the social nature of man. It repudiated the mediaeval corporate society even more radically than did the Reformation, though on the basis of secular sanctions. The alliance between Reformation and Renaissance was not envisaged by the early reformers, but it happened. And this explains much of Protestant individualism. It does not explain it all. The individualistic bias in Protestantism can also be traced back to the mediaeval period itself. It was in part an inheritance, not a discovery. The glib assertion so often heard on the lips of apologists for the mediaeval Roman sys-

[6] P. T. Forsyth, *The Principle of Authority*. Hodder & Stoughton, 1912, page 320.

tem that the social nature of the Church is wholly a Catholic monopoly is simply false. Both Protestants and Catholics have been taken by surprise as they face the secular social religions of the twentieth century.

The involvements of history, however, I must leave to one side. Whatever be the true explanation and whatever may be said of the corresponding failings in Catholicism, Protestantism is confronted by the need to recover the doctrine of the Church in the form of a doctrine of the Great Church. This, as I see it, is its most necessary task today. Wise interpreters within Protestantism itself have seen and are seeing this need. One of the most eloquent and uncompromising apologies for Protestantism that I have ever read is an essay entitled *Historical Christianity* by Alexander Vinet, a noted Swiss Reformed theologian writing a hundred years ago. I quote his frank judgment on this matter:

"The imperfection of the reforming work of the sixteenth century depends upon the doctrine of the Church not having been thoroughly gone into, or the ecclesiastical question definitely settled, when all other questions were so. This is the very point that the reformers, who could not do or see everything, have left to our care. No doubt a Church, where much is said about the Church, is not *for that reason* more vigorous or healthy; but a Church which does not realize the idea of Church, or care about realizing it, which does not even feel the need to do so, is not the most desirable Church either. Man did not separate for the sake of separating; separation was but a *medicine* that many have mistaken for *food*." [7]

The strength of Protestantism, however, lies in its possessing a principle of life which can transcend itself. It broke

[7] Alexander Vinet, *Outlines of Theology*, English Translation, London, 1866, page 423.

the bonds of tradition once. It can break them again—this time the bonds which it forged for itself during its own reign in history. To return to a Catholic idea of the Church will mean for Protestantism a supreme test of its conscience— that conscience for which it once sacrificed its ecclesiastical home and went out into a strange country. It has had much to say of repentance. It acknowledges its sins of disunity today as does no other body of Christians. If it should see its true vocation in our time and heed the call of God, a day of Pentecost might return. Dr. Paul Tillich, in a prophetic article,[8] predicts the coming of this post-Protestant "Catholic" age. It is, quite possibly, at our very door. When it is called "Catholic," this does not mean a return to the mediaeval Church—far less a submission to papal Rome. It may find its forms, indeed, in history. But it will also be a fresh creation of the Holy Spirit. That is why one may venture to speak of this rediscovered Catholicism by a new name. I call it here the "Great Church." The phrase is increasingly used. Those who employ it include in its meaning a return to the Church of history, but they also envision a great dawn.

Are there signs of its coming? Yes, there are. They may as yet be faint and traceable only in the dreams and convictions of a small minority. But minorities have determined history before.

The Ecumenical Movement

The most obvious sign of the rediscovery of the Great Church is the ecumenical movement. The very word "ecumenical" illustrates strikingly the double polarity of the call to a unified Church. For the word itself is a very old word.

[8] *The Student World*, First Quarter, 1937, pages 49 ff.

It means "universal," or "world-wide." It was once a synonym for "catholic." To our generation it is a new word.
Those who learn to use it find in it overtones of prophecy
as well as of memory. And this is exactly as it should be.

No history of the ecumenical movement can be given here.
It is scarcely a single generation old. One has to go back in
Christian history hundreds of years, a thousand years, or
even longer, to find real parallels to it. Here is the Christian
family once more "gathered." It is again a universal *ecclesia*,
an assembly. The roster of cities in which the ecumenical
conferences of our generation have met reads like a modern
version of the great Church (ecumenical) Councils of the
early centuries—Geneva (1920), Stockholm (1925), Lausanne (1927), Jerusalem (1928), Oxford (1937), Edinburgh
(1937), Madras (1938), Amsterdam (1939). From Edinburgh onward there has been in existence a World Council
of Churches. This still has its role to play in history. The
very name, however, is a carrier of promise. A world-wide
Christian community is discovering its existence, and giving
to that existence outward and visible signs. A people of
God is forming once more, seeing itself as one in time with
that people of God to which, according to an ancient story
strangely neglected, God once made promises for all time.
The twentieth century can understand again words pro-
claimed by God at the beginning of that people's history:
"I will be your God and ye shall be my people" (Lev.
26:12).

To many modern Christians the very idea of catholicity
has been utterly foreign—particularly if this idea carries
with it the assumption that to be a Christian means, first of
all, membership in a community. To be a Christian has meant
for most Protestants almost anything but churchmanship.
It has meant loyalty to ethical ideals; it has meant personal

trust in God; it has meant discipleship of Jesus; it has meant individual walking in the fear of the Lord; it has meant devotion to the Bible. All of these are precious in Christian life. These convictions and experiences were shared in parish or local church. Fellowship has never been lost in evangelical Christianity. Protestant practice has been far in advance of its ecclesiology. Yet is it exaggeration to say that most Protestants, if pressed, would have placed the idea of Church a distant second in comparison with the idea of personal commitment to Christ? The Church was not experienced vividly enough. It meant the small meeting house on the village square, often ugly, whose belittled importance was symbolized by its neglect as an outward institution. The Church as a mighty commonwealth of God, universal, holy, with a majestic history, with divine sanctions of its own superseding those of any fractional grouping—such a concept is not vividly imagined. If the ecumenical movement should bring the idea of the universal Church into the foreground of Protestant thinking once more, a revolution would loom ahead.

I may be exaggerating. Let me, however, call a witness. One of the best recent books on the ecumenical problem of our time is a volume called *Christian Reunion*, by Hugh Martin, a prominent inter-Church leader of Great Britain. The author is a Baptist. He describes autobiographically the denominational Church life of his youth—its glorious Protestant heritage, with its loyalty to the Bible, its personal piety, its fellowship of those "called out by God from humanity in general as consciously redeemed and separated to the divine service." Referring to this individualistic Christianity, he continues: "I still feel its power and own gratefully what I owe to it. But it seems to me today inadequate as a complete account of the Christian Faith. It was then a cardinal point of my creed that religion was an affair between a man and his Maker: or as Whitehead has phrased it in later years, 'Religion is what a man does with his solitariness.' In the reply to the Lausanne Conference Reports of the Wesleyan Methodists of England, there is a characteristic statement of this point of view: 'The Conference feels called upon to bear its continued and emphatic witness to the reality of immediate intercourse between God and the individual soul, and of the assurance that every man may have of his acceptance in Jesus Christ and his participation in all the fruits of the Spirit. The Conference would also stress the privilege and duty of corporate fellowship in Christ Jesus of all who are redeemed by Him.' It sounds like the individual first and the Church second, a long way second; isolated redeemed souls joining together for worship.

"That there is a truth here, I should be the last to deny. It is a bracing creed which has bred strong servants of God. But it is surely only half the truth about the Christian Faith. It was not through Baptist influence that I came to believe in any real sense in the Church except as a single congregation of worshipping people. I see now that in my own tradition there is in fact among many of its teachers a great emphasis on the universal Church and I gladly recognize that it is better stressed today. But I must in honesty state that for me it was partly through Presbyterianism and partly through Anglicanism that I entered into this realm of richer heritage of thought. The impression made by Independency upon me, and not only upon me, was so concerned with the local manifestation of the Church that I thought little in those days of that of which the local community is only the expression—the One Holy Catholic Apostolic Church, which contains not only those now alive, nor even those born since 1662, but is the general assembly and church of the first-born, and the spirits of just men made perfect, the great multitude that no man can number." [9]

Such an experience has, I am certain, found repetition in hundreds of lives. The author just quoted, however, has had unusual opportunities for ecumenical adventure. A conviction like his needs to become general. It needs to become part of the doctrinal tradition of Christian truth, and this is a slow process. It is noteworthy to recall that the hunger for a sense of the history of the Christian Church found expression at the Madras Missionary Conference. The Younger Churches felt this to be one of their most urgent needs. One of the chief tasks of the modern missionary was declared to be "to embody and transmit the experience of the Universal Church." The Report goes on to say: "We call attention of all theological and missionary training institutions to the importance for missionaries of the study of Church History —for guidance and warning from the past, for the development of a right church-consciousness in the Younger Church, and for the approach to church union." [10]

I present another witness. Few, if any, ecumenical publications contain more insight into the Church tensions of our day than does the quarterly magazine of the World's Student Christian Federation—*The Student World*. A recent article by the Chairman of the Federation, W. A. Visser 't Hooft, who is also the Secretary of the World Council of Churches, bears the title "The People of God." The writer surveys the story of God's people from the days of Abraham to our own. He finds in this story the main theme of the Bible, the people of God of the New Testament being inheritors of the promises and warnings made to those of the Old Testament—a

[9] Hugh Martin, *Christian Reunion*, Student Christian Movement Press, 1941, pages 34–36.
[10] *The Life of the Church*, Madras Series, Vol. IV, page 257.

new people, but at the same time a continuation. The story is traced through the Christian centuries—the mediaeval Church triumphing over barbarism, but losing its sense of being a *new* people, the Reformation signifying a new exodus, the Protestant churches, in their turn, capitulating before the secular forces of the modern world.

"Religion becomes a private affair. The Church becomes a point of assembly for those souls that seek their salvation along individual lines. The people of God ceases to be a people, ceases to have a recognizable identity and to form a solid community. Compare the appalling doctrine of the seventeenth century: *cuius regio, eius religio*—the prince decides the religion of his subjects—with the conception of a third race! Set the Christian of the primitive community who feels himself the member of a body which is visible as well as invisible beside the nineteenth-century Christian with his refrain '*my* religious convictions and *my* private life concern nobody'! Observe the contradiction between those divided, those atomised churches which either ignore each other or quarrel among themselves—and a people united in Christ, among whom the suffering of one member makes all suffer. Consider the distance which separates these bourgeois, solidly planted in a world of strangers, from the colonists of the Kingdom of God of which the New Testament speaks."

Then, after reviewing the rise of the giant secular social structures of our twentieth century, the author continues:

"Meanwhile the 'vacuum,' the great spiritual void of the masses has become more and more intolerable. The Church does very little to fill it. . . . It has only religious ideas to offer to men who are hungering and thirsting to be confronted with a reality that is powerful and dynamic. This is not really the Church—the people of God—conscious of belonging to the new creation, and manifesting in its life the unshakable certainty that the world is already vanquished. Need we be astonished that national messianisms gain the ear of the masses and that the doctrines of a holy people become real religions in our day? 'The people is the only end that exists,' declared the Leader of the German people. 'If the peoples perish, the religious ideas which dominate them perish too.' So God depends upon the life of people on this earth."

But the writer does not leave us with this picture of judgment and doom. Like a prophet of old, he offers hope for those who repent. "In another of those critical and decisive moments of the history of God's people, God is once more reassembling His own."

For we have the ecumenical movements of our time. Even "before the great conflicts between Church and world, God began to prepare for this great reassembling. All over the world groups of Christians, weary of their solitude and isolation, set about searching for the Church, and were forced to acknowledge in alarm that the Church in the New Testament sense no longer existed. Was the Church then to be reorganized? No, for that would only mean a careless doctoring of the wounds of the people. A little more local activity of congregations, a little more liturgy, a better system of government, the creation of ecumenical organs—all these mean nothing so long as the people of the Church have not rediscovered the full meaning of their own existence as God's people, people of the new world, a holy people, the body of Christ. Moreover, it is through heavy judgment that the people must once more relearn this ancient lesson." [11]

These are self-humbling words uttered by a leader of contemporary Protestantism. Coming from one who is at

[11] *The Student World*, Second Quarter, 1943, pages 98–101.

the same time a leader in the ecumenical movement they confront that movement with warnings also. Church reunion involves a deep-going revolution in our basic conceptions of Christianity. It means a return to the New Testament in ways many of us have not even dreamt of as yet.

The Catholic (Roman, Orthodox, Anglo-Catholic) will, to be sure, be tempted to take such a confession as that of Visser 't Hooft just quoted as a sign of a return to traditional Catholic churches. This may, in part, be true. Certainly traditional Catholicism must be taken very seriously as modern Christianity rediscovers the idea of the Great Church, of "the people of God." Yet one may doubt that such rediscovery will take quite so simple a form. Neither of the authors cited in the foregoing pages would be prepared to surrender his Protestant convictions. Both would urge that these be transcended to include a forgotten or neglected element in New Testament Christianity itself. A critical examination of historic Catholicism must wait for a later chapter. Here we are merely passing in review some signs—in the Protestant world first of all—which point to a coming Great Church, whatever be the form it will take.

The Liturgical Movement

By way of a brief mention, however, a movement within Roman Catholicism itself should be noted which also involves a rediscovery of the true New Testament Church. I refer to the Liturgical Movement. I cannot take the space to give a history of this movement even in briefest sketch. Its literature is already voluminous. It has evoked parallel movements in practically all the other Churches of Christendom. To a Protestant, the Liturgical Movement in the Roman Church seems like the Reformation come again—this time within Rome itself. If the ecumenical rediscovery of the doctrine of the Church is driving Protestants to a reëvaluation of the historic Christian centuries, here is that ecumenical rediscovery in reverse. Pages on pages in the writings of the leaders of the movement read as if they were culled out of Luther or Calvin.

For the simple fact is that the concept and actuality of a people-Church has been lost in the Roman Church also. Despite the universality and uniformity of its sway over millions of Christians, a true sense of corporateness has been lost. Worship in the Roman Church as in Protestant Churches has become individualistic. It is (I am paraphrasing Roman Catholic critics of their own Church) "devotional," not truly "liturgical." It has lost contact with common living. The leaders of the movement plead for the Mass in the vernacular, for Masses in the afternoon or evening when people can come (a privilege already largely granted, though with disciplinary protections).

The Liturgical Movement in the Roman Catholic Church is complex, and generalizations regarding it are dangerous. Yet the fact is significant that the literature of the movement finds a ready response among Protestant readers. The Protestant detects in it an approach, even within Rome, to an evangelical doctrine of the Church—a people-Church, a Church in which the "mystical Body of Christ" (a favorite phrase) is seen to be the congregation in the pews as well as the host on the altar. Spokesmen for the movement recommend the more frequent use of the name Holy Supper for the Mass, since this describes its corporate nature.[12] The modern neglect of congregational participation in the Mass is deplored—the worshippers "attending" Mass, but indulg-

[12] See the article *The Breaking of Bread*, by Donald Atwater, in *Orate Fratres*, Jan. 21, 1940.

ing in individualistic prayer, each one following the devices of his own heart, and often neglectful of his neighbor.

The almost exclusive concentration of devotional attention upon the sacred elements in the Eucharist is seen as a mistake. Sacraments are corporate *acts* of the Church. Dom Odo Casel, Abbot of Maria Laach, and one of the authoritative scholars of the Movement defines the Catholic Mass as ". . . a symbolic *act* which is imbued with the *presence* of the redemptive *act*." The Church "through the solemn words of commemoration (the anamnesis) makes the *sacrifice* of Christ and thereby the redemptive *work* which culminated in his death to be *present*." [13] Here, clearly, is a view of the Eucharist far removed from that familiar in most Roman Catholic formularies. It undercuts the tortured controversies on transsubstantiation. The very word sacrament is interpreted once more as a "holy action" in place of merely a "holy thing." The Real Presence of Christ in the Holy Supper becomes the "making present" of the redeeming sacrifice on the cross, the showing forth of "the Lord's *death* till he come." Rudolf Otto, in an essay on the Holy Supper from a Protestant point of view, cites Dom Casel's definition of the Mass and accepts it as his own. He adds the striking comment: "The words of the Catholic writer may permit one to hope that, on the strength of this interpretation, the separated denominations may yet find some common ground in a part of their doctrine and practice which is now such a painful source of estrangement between them." [14]

Here is but a brief glimpse into the literature of the Liturgical Movement in the Roman Church. Anyone familiar with the history of religious controversy of the past four hundred years must rub his eyes in amazement. The liturgy

[13] See article *Messe* in the second volume of the encyclopaedia *Die Religion in Geschichte und Gegenwart*.

[14] Rudolf Otto, *Religious Essays*, Oxford, 1937, page 52.

is not all of Christian life, but it is crucial. In the area of liturgical symbols the bitterest battles have been fought. The very words most familiar in the Protestant and Catholic liturgical traditions have become opposing war cries—Mass as over against Lord's Supper, surplice or chasuble as over against gown, sacrifice as over against communion. Can it be that this ancient field of strife may once more see a peace —a peace not of capitulation or empty compromise, but a peace resulting from a rediscovery of the corporate fellowship in Christ which alone gives the Church's liturgical life its meaning? For if the literature of the Roman Liturgical Movement reads as if the Reformation had come alive again, the corresponding liturgical movements in Protestantism look as if the Reformation Churches were rediscovering, in their turn, the forgotten centuries antedating the great revolt. Symbols out of the worship life of the early historic Church are reappearing once more—altars and vestments, candles and chancel lights, the Christian Year, and the beauty of holiness in place of the cult of the unadorned. In themselves these matters of cult may be of minor import, but they indicate a change of mood. Not all of Church history from the sixth century to the sixteenth need any longer be labelled the reign of Antichrist.

Enough, however, has been said about the liturgical movements of our time to indicate that in these we have another sign of the coming of the One Great Church. The ecumenical movement is such a sign; the liturgical movement is a second.

The Return to Orthodoxy

A third sign—possibly the most important of all—is the revolution which is taking place in contemporary theology. This revolution is not easy to label by a word or a phrase. The names which are most frequently being applied to it are

"Neo-orthodoxy," or "Biblical theology." The title of a recent book which describes in autobiographical form this new movement expresses its genius. The title is *On to Orthodoxy*.[15] The phrase evidences the same double polarity which we met in the ecumenical movement—a return which is also an advance.

The world of contemporary intellectual culture is as yet little aware of this epoch-making shift in Christian thought. Theology, once the queen of the sciences, has long been dethroned. The very word "theology" is culturally almost taboo. The modern university scarcely recognizes it. Yet sooner or later, let us hope, the intellectual rediscovery of Christianity of our generation will be recognized and gain a hearing. The university world had, indeed, some excuse a generation ago for neglecting Protestant theology, since this had come close to a capitulation before secular learning. This excuse does not exist today.

In dealing with this return to Orthodoxy, we are again within the Protestant fold. There are no analogues, or very few, in Catholicism. Roman Catholicism can claim that it never departed from Orthodoxy and therefore is called to no return. Define Orthodoxy in purely Catholic terms and the claim can be granted. But Catholic pride is a little out of place. A great war has been fought and won on the battlefield of modern thought. The Roman Catholic has had little share in it.

> Gilead abode beyond the Jordan:
> And Dan, why did he remain in ships?
> Asher sat still at the haven of the sea
> And abode by his creeks.
>
> —*Judges 5:17*

[15] D. R. Davies, *On to Orthodoxy*, Hodder, 1939.

Rome, for hundreds of years, has been Christianity in a mediaeval fortress. She has remained entrenched and outwardly unconquered. There is no question that she preserved Christianity in a purer form than that which Protestantism could show in some of its decadent recent manifestations. But Rome has not shared in the conflict. She cannot thrill to the cry of victory—"*On* to Orthodoxy."

We are too close to our time to write history wisely. Yet for the majority of thoughtful Christians of the twentieth century what has happened in the realm of Christian theology should be a story of consuming interest. It may be nothing short of the salvation of the Christian Faith for modern man.

From the Reformation onward, Protestantism has been exposed to the onslaught of modernist thought. At first, with the great revolt itself behind them, the Reformation churches enjoyed a period of stabilization. They had the Bible and such Church institutions as they had carried over from the long Christian past. Continuity was a mark of the Protestant schism quite as much as discontinuity. But these institutionalized safeguards were not Protestantism's chief reliance. This was the Bible. The Bible always seemed safe—and the Faith based on the Bible—a Faith which linked the sixteenth century with the great age of the early Church. The Renaissance did not at first undermine this faith. Nor did the terrible religious wars of the seventeenth century. These merely set confessions more firmly against one another. But then came the Enlightenment of the eighteenth century, with its trust in reason. Protestant pietism sprang up as an antidote, and has remained a spiritual anchorage for millions of Christian souls ever since, even through the storms of the nineteenth century.

For the storms came. Science emancipated itself from

traditional controls. Evolutionary hypotheses became dogmas universally accepted, usually with uncritical abandon.
The Romantic Movement in literature and art revolted
against the decorum and checks of the "great tradition" of
classical-Christian culture. Rousseau ruled supreme as the
new prophet of emancipation. This romantic gospel freed
man from the burden of personal responsibility for evil. The
age-old Christian doctrine of original sin, along with the
similar classical view of man as a being rooted in the sin of
pride, gave way before the glorification of man as good by
nature. Evil must be henceforth traced to society. Most of
us have been brought up in this new climate of moral optimism and scarcely realize what a gulf separates us from all
earlier centuries of civilized man. The contrast can be found
epitomized in a quotation from Carlyle.

"Alas, no, M. Roux!" Carlyle exclaims, referring to Rousseau, and to the social overturn of the French Revolution,
"A Gospel of Brotherhood not according to any of the four
old Evangelists and calling on men to repent, and amend
each his own wicked existence, that they might be saved; but
a Gospel rather, as we often hint, according to a new fifth
Evangelist Jean-Jacques, calling on men to amend *each the
whole world's* wicked existence and be saved by making the
Constitution—a thing different and distant *toto coelo*." [16]

But not only did the general climate of thought suffer a
profound revolution. The citadel of Christian Faith itself
was attacked. The Bible, its chief symbol in the Protestant
world, could not escape the judgments of modern scientific
enlightenment. We have had a century now of historical
scrutiny of this ancient holy Book. Most of us are sufficiently
familiar with the lingering Bible Fundamentalisms of our day
to realize what Protestantism has gone through. The modern

[16] Quoted in Irving Babbitt, *Democracy and Leadership*, Houghton
Mifflin, 1924, page 7.

schoolboy knows that he cannot believe the Bible as his grandfather did. Hence his ignorance does not much bother his conscience. The Bible has become a book like any other book, an ancient book out of a dead past. He may be willing enough to revere it as a classic—one of a long series of archaeological literary remains of which he is contentedly unaware. (A schoolboy once defined a classic as a book which would not be read unless it were studied in *class!*)

The dilemma which has confronted thousands of modern Christians has been tragic. This is true particularly of those whose childhood home was still one in the simple pietistic tradition and who then met the disillusionments of critical intellectual reason in university and college. They had to choose, so they thought, between the integrity of the intellect and their heritage of naïve faith. The institutional Church had been overthrown as ultimate authority at the Reformation. Now the Bible as literal authority was gone also. To launch forth on an individualistic voyage of discovery of ultimate truth beckoned to some, but proved usually too great a burden. The average educated modern has lived, accordingly, on scraps and remnants of a torn faith and a broken tradition. The increasing number of conversions to Rome in our time is not surprising. Here is tradition still majestically incarnate. The phenomenal growth of Anglo-Catholicism finds explanation also in the débâcle of authoritarian Protestant Christianity. Anglo-Catholicism uniquely combined a rebirth of the doctrine of an institutional Church with a willingness to adjust itself to critical scholarship in the Biblical field.

One alternative to complete surrender to intellectual scepticism however, has not yet been mentioned. It proved for a brief time the most successful of all. Insofar as enlightened Protestantism maintained itself in recent generations, it found in this alternative a temporary haven. It has already a name in history. It is called Liberal Protestantism. A better name may be simply Modernism. These names are misleading if taken as descriptions, since the return to Orthodoxy of contemporary Christian thought, while it reacts violently against Liberal Protestantism, retains many of its "liberal" and even "modern" characteristics. Honest Christianity can never return again to the authoritarian literal Bible. To that extent the nineteenth century has won an irreversible victory.

The solution of Liberal Protestantism for the dilemma of modern Christianity seemed at first absurdly simple and satisfying. Historical and scientific scholarship had robbed the Bible of its absoluteness. Very well. But that same critical scholarship had brought into relief the historical itself. Miracles might vanish. The mysterious beliefs *about* Christ of the Pauline epistles and of the Christian creeds might be thought-forms of a dead past. The Old Testament might be merely the record of a primitive people's evolution from barbarism to a moral faith. But one rock remained, the Jesus central in this long history—a Jesus human, appealing, with a teaching above the relativities of history. Why should this not suffice?

At first contact a thrilling discovery! The Epistle to the Romans which, since Luther's day, had been thought to contain the heart of the Bible could now be relegated to an appendix. The Sermon on the Mount could take its place. The Jesus of these matchless chapters could capture the allegiance of the believer. The rest of the Gospel story merely illustrated, in parable and healing acts, this ethic of humanitarian Love. The Cross was a dramatic climax to the biographical drama of Jesus' life. The Gospel was, in fact, a hero-story. Faith became loyalty to the "hero," to his teaching. Practical discipleship could at last replace academic theology. A social gospel could now supplement individualistic piety, a carrying out of the ethic of love into the world of men. Morality could replace the long reign of doctrine. Christians at the turn of the twentieth century thrilled to Matthew Arnold's simple definition of religion—"morality touched with emotion." If the older doctrinal language about Christ was still held to be precious, much of it could be subsumed under the new ethical creeds. One might still talk easily enough of Incarnation or Atonement or Resurrection or Salvation. Give these words an ethical content and they became at once simple and easy to grasp. Nor was the concept "Church" meaningless in the new version of the Christian Faith. The Church was the company of those who subscribed to the ideals of Jesus and put them into practice. It was the society called to build the Kingdom of God on earth.

But further descriptions of this "new" Christianity are probably not necessary. It is still the popular Christianity of enlightened Protestantism today and can be met on any Sunday in most American Churches. Reduced to secular idealism, it is the prevailing philosophy of our time in our public schools. No one living today—not even the Catholic in his fortress—is uninfluenced by it.

Within the past generation, however, a great revolt has taken place against this modernist Christianity. For, as the modern world marched into the twentieth century, this optimistic, progressive Christianity broke under the strain of tragic events. The First World War marked a great turning point. How can the mere preaching of ethical ideals control the wild will of man? Men by nature simply do not love one another, and merely telling them that they *ought* to love will not produce the power of performance. A wholly unrealistic view of human nature was discovered to underlie the reduced Christianity of Liberalism. In the face of Nazi barbarism, even the recently despised Christian doctrine of original sin made more practical sense. The appeal of Christianity as a beautiful hero-story was seen to be no substitute for an honest dealing with the God of conscience or of history. The modernized version of Christianity could almost be described as "Christianity without God." Bring God—the God of the Bible—back into the picture, and the trust in "morality touched with emotion" could be seen as a sentimental dream, unreal even in man's wrestling with the demons in his own soul.

Furthermore, historical scholarship dealing with the Bible, which at first seemed to validate a human Jesus religion, turned against its own offspring. Jesus, pictured as a teacher of humanitarian ethics, if viewed by a more penetrating analysis, never existed. He is a creation of sentimental imagination. The Gospels are not "hero-story" biographies. The Sermon on the Mount, read in its context, is not a blue-print of ethical progress which men merely need to admire in order to achieve. Read against the background of the Old Testament, with its fear of the God of the Law, the Sermon on the Mount is far more like a dress-rehearsal of Judgment Day. It confronts man with the unachievable holiness of Deity. Repentance, not achievement, is the first response.

Modernist Christianity saw itself confronted by an impasse. It could repudiate the Bible altogether and become a disembodied humanism, or it would, in some way, in order to be Christianity at all, have to return to tradition—to Orthodoxy. Could this return be achieved without treachery to intellectual conscience, and without repudiating the positive achievements of Renaissance, Enlightenment, science, and historical criticism? Could there be a "modern" Orthodoxy?

Well, such an Orthodoxy is here. It is still in its infancy.

Yet hundreds of Christian scholars and theological students are already breathing the bracing air of a rediscovered Biblical Christianity. The story of the rebirth of belief in the Bible is as yet little known outside the halls of theological learning. A decadent Protestantism still reigns in much contemporary Church life. It will soon wither and die. Grievous has been the hurt of the daughter of God's people. An entire generation or more has grown up, even within the Churches, who have never heard the true Christian Gospel. But, to use military metaphor, the lines have somehow held. A reborn Christianity can march forth to victory, unafraid any longer of the giants of secularism. The army is a Gideon's army now, a minority. The era of alliance between Church and world may be over. Yet the future, outwardly dark, can be faced with a new courage.

To describe this new Orthodoxy at any length is not possible here. One clue to its solution of the problem of the Bible is, however, very simple. The sacred Christian Book had been robbed of its divinity. It was thought of as a history book—a human history book. Nineteenth-century criticism had subjected the Bible to historical scrutiny. Very well. Push the scrutiny to its conclusions and the Bible discloses a story, a drama of amazing proportions and meaning. Jesus remains at the center of the story, but He must be seen in perspective. The Bible must be read as a whole or not at all. It was written by members of a community of Faith, and can be understood only *in* Faith. The Book telling the story, however, is not the story itself. The Book may be full of human relativities, misunderstandings, legends, myths. Once interpreted from within the community of Faith in which it appeared, it is seen to contain a Revelation from outside of history. God is the chief actor, not man. Man can only respond to God's "mighty acts," as He commands, judges, and then Himself appears in history—coming down from heaven—and redeems man through a mysterious death and resurrection.

Christian Faith may be as difficult under this rediscovered view of the Bible as it was in earlier eras. The point is, however, that Faith is also just as easy. Faith in the divinity of the Book may have gone. Faith in the God whose Word speaks through the Book may be clearer than ever.

A critic (I do not know the name) has put into epigrammatic form the contrast between the devitalized Christianity of recent modernism and the Christianity of Biblical revelation. Every child in a Christian Sunday School used to memorize, as summary of the Christian faith, a verse from the Gospel of St. John (3:16): "God so loved the world, that He gave His only begotten Son, that whosoever believeth on Him should not perish, but have eternal life." These are words full of mystery. Evidently a great story lies behind them—a story involving eternity and time, and the ultimates of death and human destiny. Modernist Christianity, if true to the logic of its gospel, would have to rewrite this New Testament verse to read: "God so loved the world that He once inspired a certain Jew to inform His contemporaries that there is a great deal to be said for loving one's neighbor." Unfair satire, no doubt, but expressive of an essential gulf between virtually two religions.

The preceding pages have furnished only a passing glimpse into the theological revolution sweeping across the Protestant world today. The sketch has been brief since our theme is not this revolution itself but its meaning for Christian unity. Has it significance for the coming Great Church?

It has great meaning—quite possibly greater meaning than the ecumenical movements of our time themselves. It has saved Protestantism. And Protestantism is needed for the

Church of the future. An observer of Christianity at the turn of the twentieth century might have predicted that Catholicism would soon be the only form of Christianity left. Yet this would have been a Christianity which had refused to face modern thought. It must never be forgotten that Roman Catholicism is still Fundamentalist in its view of the Bible. This may look like strength, but it is tragic weakness. The battle for preserving the Bible for the modern world has been a Protestant battle—and has led to a Protestant victory. Catholicism itself may, under the rule of God over His universal Church, some day thank her belittled rival for protecting the rock upon which she, too, in spite of all of her doctrines of the papacy, is built—the Bible.

No Christian unity can be other than a community of faith. Without a shared faith, the concept of "Church" is ultimately meaningless. Christian faith must rest on acts of God beyond or previous to the Church herself. There is no such resting place other than the revelation of God in history enshrined in the Bible. Its recovery, therefore, was and is a prerequisite for Christian reunion.

Protestantism's revival, to be sure, will heighten, for a time, the Catholic-Protestant schism. From this point of view, healing that schism may be delayed. Protestantism will not now capitulate. But the recovery, for the modern man, of faith in Biblical revelation has at least one implication that leads straight on to the recovery of faith in the Church —the Great Church. For the Bible is seen now to need the community of Faith. The Bible, as an historically conditioned book, cannot stand by itself. The Book is not yet Christianity. The community of Faith can be Christianity. Only within that faith can the Bible be Revelation. The community of Faith is the Church.

Bible Christianity and Church Christianity have faced

each other across a chasm for centuries. They were not
meant thus to be divorced. In the Bible they are joined, for
the Bible is itself Church-religion. Is it too much to hope
that Bible Christianity and Church Christianity can again
meet and become one? Such a reunion will not take place
without great tribulations. The divided Christianities will
each be compelled to submit to judgment. Bible Christianity
will have to rediscover the centrality of the Church of God
in the Holy Scriptures themselves. Church Christianity will
have to yield its pretensions of being a substitute for the
Redemption wrought "once for all" by God Himself. But
God still rules in history. The Church is a community of
expectancy. Let a mood of expectancy penetrate the slum-
bering people of God and the miracle of the reborn Great
Church can happen. "And it shall be said in that day, Lo,
this is our God; we have waited for him, and he will save
us: this is the Lord; we have waited for him, we will be glad
and rejoice in his salvation" (Is. 25:9).

II

THE CHURCH OF CHRISTIAN FAITH

What is the Church? Every Christian would have some answer. Without "Church" of some sort there would be no Christians. Yet most modern Christians would not find it easy to give a definition of "Church" which more than a fraction of the other Christians in the world would accept. The concept of the Church is, in fact, one of the most difficult in Christian experience. Even theologians may not quite know what it means or ought to mean.

"I believe one Catholic and Apostolic Church." This is the familiar phrase of the common Christian creed. "Almost every word of the sentence," says Emil Brunner, a contemporary Swiss theologian, "is incomprehensible for the present-day man and even for the average Christian. Luther called the word Church a 'blank,' and would have preferred the term 'the Christian folk.' 'Church' means for most people the great building with the tower and chimes where every Sunday services of worship are conducted. All of that, to be sure, is used by the Church and reminds us that the matter of greatest significance in the Church is the proclamation of the Gospel. But the misunderstanding is just as great." [1]

Misunderstandings and confusions as regards the meaning of the word "Church" are not limited to the man in the street. Christian history is shot through with them. Consider the author whom I have just quoted. The whole body of Christians calling itself Catholic would not be able to admit

[1] Emil Brunner, *Our Faith*, Scribner, 1936, page 7.

that he was himself fully a member of the Church. They might honor him as a man and as a scholar and concede him the adjective Christian. But he is a Protestant. And Protestants are not "Church." In the ecumenical movement the term "Church" is beginning to find frequent use. In Catholic eyes it is thus used improperly always. The Protestant, in his turn, while he is usually more inclusive in his application of tests of Church membership, is equally puzzled when he deals with a Catholic Church like Rome. What, so he is forced to ask, can the idea of "Church" mean in a system ruled by a pope who by definition stands outside the Church itself. Papal pronouncements, so says a decree of the Vatican Council, must be held to be irreformable "without consent of the Church" (*ex sese, non autem ex consensu ecclesiae*).

And if a student, puzzled by these and other controversies surrounding the idea of the Church, seeks guidance in the traditional doctrinal systems of Christian thought, he will be amazed to find here a curious vacuum. Books on every other Christian doctrine fill whole libraries. But where are books on the doctrine of the Church? There is the New Testament. Then there is the *City of God* of Augustine. But what else—until almost our own generation? Of course, the vacuum is not complete. The Apostolic and early Church Fathers, for example, frequently mention the Church, Belief in the Church became an article of the Christian Creed. But a gulf already exists between the New Testament and the Hellenic Christianity even of the early centuries. Harnack, the great historian of doctrine, bluntly says that the Apostolic tradition as regards the New Testament idea of the Church "very soon, comparatively speaking, became obsolete or lost its power to influence. Even the Apologists make little use of it. Augustine was the first to return to it." [2]

[2] Harnack, *History of Dogma*, English translation, vol. 1, page 153.

Turn to the mediaeval scholastics, who might at least have had Augustine as a model. The doctrine of the Church is scarcely mentioned. The *Summa* of St. Thomas Aquinas has a brief chapter on Christ or Pope as head of the Church. But that is virtually all—and to a questioner quite unsatisfying. An article in the most recent theological encyclopaedia can say openly: "Scholasticism scarcely ever dealt with the doctrine of the Church. What it had to say it subsumed under the treatment of Christ as Head of the Church or under the topic of the sacrament of ordination." On the doctrine of the Church in Roman theology generally the same scholar can say: "There exists in the Catholic Church of today no real dogma concerning the Church. Instead, the Catholic Church constitutes herself as the presupposition for all dogma." [3]

Do we not meet in this doctrinal vacuum of the Hellenic and mediaeval tradition one of the strangest of history's paradoxes? The Roman Church, in western Christendom, has laid claim for four hundred years to a monopoly of Church-Christianity. Protestants, including Anglicans, are simply excommunicated. Yet Rome has no dogma of the Church—except herself. The astounding strength of such a naïve position is obvious. Historical fact becomes dogma, as did once the mighty acts of Biblical Revelation. Hence the historical Church itself becomes Revelation. The tension between Bible and Church is resolved in favor of the latter, even though lip service may still be paid to the priority of the Bible. The Church escapes judgment. On this issue Rome and the Reformation Churches confront one another across a wide chasm.

For, unless Rome's position is accepted, a doctrine of the Church becomes a necessity. The Churches excommunicated

[3] *Religion in Geschichte und Gegenwart.* Article *Kirche* III.

by Rome and seeking a Church-Christianity of their own need such a doctrine desperately. At the Reformation, doctrines of the Church did appear. Every Reformation confession has one. In comparison with the silence on the doctrine of the Church on the part of scholastic theology, the Reformation marks, indeed, a revival. The nineteenth of the Thirty-Nine Articles of the Church of England is a succinct summary of many Reformation confessions. "The visible Church of Christ is a congregation of faithful men, in the which the pure Word of God is preached, and the Sacraments be duly ministered according to Christ's ordinance, in all things that of necessity are requisite to the same. As the Church of Jerusalem, Alexandria, and Antioch have erred; so also the Church of Rome hath erred, not only in their living and manner of ceremonies, but also in matters of Faith." The acknowledgment of a norm for the Church other than the Church herself was surely a momentous step for Reformation thought. Yet could anyone assert that this, or similar confessions (even disregarding the problem raised by the words "visible Church") are adequate as a doctrine of the Church for the solving of our ecumenical problems today?

Emil Brunner has a good criticism of Reformed doctrine. On the familiar formula in Reformation confessions for discerning a true Church, he says: "It is certainly of little value to consider pure doctrine and correct administration of the Sacraments as such characteristics (of the Church). . . . The false, one-sided objective concept of the Church is certainly also to blame for the Church's no longer understanding itself as a missionary Church. The reduction to two of the criteria for the true Church given us in the New Testament, and indeed to the two which offer themselves most easily to objectivisation, namely, pure doctrine and correct administration of the Sacraments, resulted in the period following in a tremendous impoverishment of the Church." [4] It is indeed a strange fact that no Church creed or confession has hitherto made more than passing use of the rich symbolism descriptive of the Church which fills the New Testament.

The impression usually accepted without investigation that Catholic dogma is rich in doctrines of the Church is simply an illusion. But a vacuum exists in Protestant theological thinking on the Church also. To work out a doctrine of the Church may have been a task assigned precisely to our era in Christian history. Ours is, in some ways, the first age called upon to formulate an ecumenical theology. The Reformation return to the Bible must lead eventually to the Church as well as to the Bible. For the Bible is not silent on the Church. "For the Church the world was made," says one of the earliest documents of Christian literature.[5] Our familiar hymn is quite Biblical when it sings of Christ Himself:

> From Heaven he came and sought her
> To be his holy bride;
> With his own blood he bought her,
> And for her life he died.[6]

The strange vacuum in Christian doctrine regarding the Church deserves, however, an attempt at explanation. In part a valid explanation is that which is implied by the silence in Roman dogma. The Church is a living thing. How can it

[4] Emil Brunner, *The Divine-Human Encounter*, Westminster Press, 1943, pages 189–200. Luther and Calvin make far more of the Church than is admitted in Catholic polemic literature. The Reformers' views have been neatly summarized in J. S. Whale's *Christian Doctrine*, Macmillan, 1942, pages 144–149.

[5] *Shepherd of Hermas* 2.4.1.

[6] The remarkable popularity of the hymn *The Church's One Foundation*, from which the above is a quotation, may indicate a deeper awareness in our time of the true nature of the Church than modernist individualism might lead one to expect.

really describe itself? Life must cease before the anatomist can dissect and analyze. It was not until the eighteenth century that medical science discovered the circulation of the blood. Yet the blood of physicians themselves had been in circulation from the dawn of medicine. The Church, regardless of poverty of doctrine regarding herself, simply exists. The Holy Spirit, third person of the Trinity, abides in her. By her fruits she is known, not by the abstractions of theologians. Yet the argument, valid as it may be, proves too much. The New Testament Church, too, was alive, but the New Testament Church wrote the Epistle to the Ephesians and much else about herself. Furthermore, a divided Church, one in which the very word "Church" is withheld among Christians, cannot live any longer in uncritical indifference of doctrinal clarification. Rome accomplishes such naïve aloofness from doctrinal self-examination only through blind pride. And Rome, too, is awaking to the need of knowing herself to be part of the mystical body of Christ, as the Liturgical Movement happily indicates.

A more searching explanation of the vacuum on the subject of the Church in Christian thought may lie in the fact that Jewish Christianity vanished so early, leaving Hellenic Christianity alone to spread through the Roman world. This meant the loss of the Hebraic view of religion. All Christian doctrine has suffered from this loss of the Hebraic worldview. The early Church fought a manful battle against Hellenism, it is true. The historic Christian Creeds are an evidence of this great struggle, and Frederick Denison Maurice was largely right in declaring that at the close of the period of warfare: "The Church was Hebraic despite of itself." [7] Yet the Church emerged lamed by the struggle. The

[7] F. D. Maurice, *Moral and Metaphysical Philosophy*, Macmillan, 1872, vol. i, page 397.

full understanding of the Biblical story of God's revelation has never reëmerged in Christian thought until our own day. The Biblical theology of the rediscovered Orthodoxy of our generation will have much to teach us, as it brings to light the forgotten treasures of the Bible.

Nowhere is the loss of the Hebraic, Biblical view of Christianity more tragic than in an early loss of the doctrine of the Church. The Old Testament, in particular, suffered neglect. Yet for an understanding of the Church, the Old Testament is crucial. "The Gentile Church, though it reverenced the Old Testament as at first its only Bible, and refused to abandon it at the call of Marcion, was little able fully to understand it. It possessed in the early ages hardly any Hebrew scholar except St. Jerome; and it is only in comparatively modern days that the Hebrew outlook has come to be understood." [8]

The author just cited goes on to show how both Greeks and Romans, despite their great gifts, could not guide in understanding the Church. They had not been through the long centuries of discipline as a "chosen people." The very word "ecclesia"—the chosen band, the called—had for Greeks and Romans secular, not holy, connotations. "The amount of harm which has been done to the Church by Greek intellectualism and Roman autocracy is incalculable. Back then to the Hebrews!" [9]

For if we turn to the Bible, with the Old Testament not ignored, the doctrine of the Church meets us on almost every

[8] H. L. Goudge, *The Church of England and Reunion*, Society for Promoting Christian Knowledge, 1938, page 84. My argument in these paragraphs owes much to this book. Other books which are bringing the Old Testament Church back into the picture of Biblical Christianity are A. G. Hebert's *The Throne of David*, Faber, 1941; and Phythian-Adams' *The People and the Presence*, Oxford, 1942.

[9] H. L. Goudge, *The Church of England and Reunion*, Society for Promoting Christian Knowledge, 1938, page 85.

page. The very title-page of the Bible—the Book "containing the Old and New Testaments"—marks it as a book about "Churches." Testament means covenant, and covenant, to the Hebrew mind, meant a relationship bestowed upon a chosen people by a gracious God. Personal religion, as we moderns have come to call it, is not ruled out, of course, as many familiar psalms prove, but no Hebrew ever dreamt of personal religion except within the corporate covenant. Nor is this corporate relationship with God as the framework of salvation lost in the New Testament. Here again we meet only Church. Entrance requirements had altered, that is all. The "chosen people" were now a new Israel, open to all who believe "good news" and repent and are baptized. But of a lessening of the corporate nature of the covenant with God, there is no hint. To his contemporaries the new covenant brought by Jesus was not discontinuous with the old, but its fulfillment. His coming seemed the end of all things, history's scroll complete.

The Bible as a "Church Book" is a unit and a whole. It is "the story of the mighty acts of God, winning for Himself a people (before Christ) and through that people (after Christ) reconciling the whole world with Himself." [10] And if that story is read with our Church of the twentieth century in mind, how it illumines our contemporary problems! The choosing of that ancient *ecclesia*, is a mystery, as is our being chosen today. They were an unprepossessing people. "The Lord thy God giveth thee not this good land for thy righteousness; for thou art a stiff-necked people" (Deut. 9:6). They scarcely ever proved fully worthy of God's choice. Yet they remained a people holy unto God. Rebellion, apostasy, punishment, redemption—all followed one

[10] G. E. Phillips, *The Old Testament in the World Church*, Lutterworth, 1942, page 149.

another as the story proceeds. The burden of being God's chosen seemed too much for them. Only a remnant remained true to Him. Yet the covenant on God's side was not broken. At the begining of the Exile, Jeremiah can have God say: "The people which were left of the sword found grace in the wilderness: even Israel, when I went to cause him to rest. . . . I have loved thee with an everlasting love" (Jer. 31).

God concentrated on an increasingly smaller remnant. Finally a single Figure appeared, carrier alone of the burden and the promise of God's covenant with His people—the Messiah, the Christ. In Him the old covenant was fulfilled and a new covenant was born. He was the bridge between the two. The point is, however, that the new covenant is still a covenant with a people. A modern Biblical scholar can say with truth: "When the Messiah was in the tomb, Israel was in the tomb. . . . When Christ rose, the Church rose from the dead." [11]

This Church of the New Testament, therefore, is a continuation, but also a new creation of God. It is now a universal Church, a catholic Church. Gentiles can become members. But the concept of Church as a visible corporate body is never lost. The idea of an *invisible* Church is foreign to the Bible. Hence salvation in the New Testament is never thought of as an affair merely between God and an individual. A man was either in or out of the new *ecclesia*, just as he had been either a Jew or a non-Jew. To be a member of the Church did not, of course, guarantee "salvation" in an individual sense—any more than it had for the people of the Old Testament. To be a member meant to be one of the called or chosen, and that might subject an individual to

[11] L. S. Thornton, *The Common Life in the Body of Christ*, Dacre Press, 1943, page 282.

judgment far more severe than any meted out to a pagan. The Church was the carrier of a promise and of a presence. Membership in the Church signified sharing in the promise and living in the presence. How the individual Christian responded to the privileges and demands of Church membership was a different story. St. Paul writes with utter frankness how in the Church of Corinth there is "such fornication as is not so much as named among the Gentiles" (1 Cor. 5:1). Yet this same Church is called the body of Christ and the temple of the Holy Spirit (1 Cor. 3:16; 12:27). This contradiction between corporate holiness and individual unholiness has been a source of confusion for Christians for centuries. Hundreds of sects have arisen in Christian history through an attempt to avoid the contradiction, by limiting membership to proven "saints." The doctrine of an invisible Church tries to resolve the same contradiction. Yet the solution is fairly clear when we draw upon the analogy of the Old Testament Church. "You only have I known of all the families of the earth: therefore I will punish you for all your iniquities," says the prophet Amos (3:2). St. Paul voices threats of damnation to the Corinthian Christians in connection with the Lord's Supper—"For he that eateth and drinketh unworthily, eateth and drinketh damnation to himself" (1 Cor. 11:29). But it would not have occurred either to Amos or to St. Paul to recommend recourse to salvation outside this sinning Church, or to attempt to found a new Church. The Church for both is a corporate body with which God is in a peculiar relationship. This relationship, or covenant, is an objective fact, regardless of whether man's response to it is a worthy or an unworthy one.

The Church of the New Testament is portrayed as a continuation of the old Israel. Yet it is also new. It is the new "remnant" which Jesus gathered and to which He committed new responsibilities, new gifts, a new relationship with God through Himself. Particularly, as we read the story of the founding of the new *ecclesia* after the Resurrection and Ascension of Christ, this new people of God is distinguished by the gift of the Holy Spirit.

Whether Jesus, in His earthly ministry, actually founded the Christian Church can be debated among scholars. Some important issues depend upon the answers accepted. The Roman Church goes back for its sanctions to a literal interpretation of the words addressed to Peter—"Upon this rock I will build my church" (Matt. 16:18). Protestant scholars reject such an interpretation and even express doubts whether Jesus ever used the word "Church" at all, despite its appearance in the Matthean Gospel.[12] The background of the Old Testament helps to clarify the historical question. The Christian Church began in the midst of the Hebrew Church. It began with the call of the first disciples. Jesus "called them out in order that through them and on them He might lay the foundation stone of a new edifice. . . . He gathered His own, the people that were 'His,' and in them He planted the consciousness that they were a separate community. The question whether Jesus Himself founded the Church may be answered in the affirmative, not only in the dogmatic sense but in the historical sense. He founded the New Convenant, not as an *ecclesia invisibilis*, as those who regard the Church purely as an invisible spiritual body would have us believe, but as a real community, a people, however unassuming it may have seemed at first, whose constitution is 'the blood of the New Covenant.' "[13]

Nevertheless, however far back the story of the Christian

[12] The best discussion I know on this whole question is in Flew, *Jesus and His Church*, Abingdon, 1938. See particularly, pages 123–135.

[13] Emil Brunner, *The Mediator*, Macmillan, 1934, pages 558–559.

Church can be traced, the coming of the Holy Spirit at Pentecost marks a beginning also. Through the remaining period of Church history covered by the New Testament account, the Christian Church is a new "mighty act" of God. It is the Spirit-bearing community.

What did this mean? No reader of the New Testament can doubt that any Biblical doctrine of the Church must come to terms with the fact and the doctrine of the Holy Spirit.

The Holy Spirit and the Church

We enter here upon a confusion of tongues in the history of Christian thought. If the doctrine of the Church is today still something of an unexplored doctrine, the doctrine of the Holy Spirit, while not unexplored, is in an equally puzzling state. "With respect to the Holy Spirit, there has not been as yet, on the part of learned and distinguished investigators of the Scriptures, a discussion of the subject full enough and careful enough to make it possible for us to obtain an intelligent conception of His proper individuality." That sentence was written by St. Augustine in the fifth century.[14] It might still be written today. "What the modern Church makes of the Spirit," says T. R. Glover in his *Paul of Tarsus* (page 218), "when it is not merely reciting quotations, it is hard to say; very little might be the answer, if we were to tell the truth. . . . One great theologian of our day says bluntly that no original work has been done on the Holy Spirit since the days of the Apostles." This blight on the doctrine of the Holy Spirit seems to have paralleled the similar blight on the doctrine of the Church. It may have had the same cause—a loss of insight into the Hebraic sense of

[14] *De Fide et Symbolo*, Chap. 9, sec. 19.

a corporate covenant with God. Certainly it is found early
in Hellenic Christianity. "That the Holy Spirit had been
poured out upon the Church," says a competent historian
of the ancient Church, "was realized by the early post-
apostolic writers; but they do not appear to have connected
the fact with the Lord's promise of another Paraclete or
with the event of Pentecost. Even the Apologists of the
second century refer but seldom and vaguely to the Pentecostal gift." [15]

A full treatment of what tradition has to say about the
doctrine of the Holy Spirit cannot, however, be attempted
here. As with the doctrine of the Church, the Reformation
certainly marked a great revival. And our generation, with
its rediscovery of insight into the Bible, may mark an era
of further rich discoveries.

I venture the suggestion that the doctrine of the Holy
Spirit in Christian tradition suffers from several ambiguities
in the use of terms. I name two:

First: The meaning of the word "spirit" in ordinary
speech. We use the word to describe the element in man
which is contrasted with "body." It is an immanent, individualist, psychological fact. But we also use the word "spirit"
very differently—to describe, not a phenomenon in individual psychology, but in social life. We speak freely of the
"spirit" of a school or a college, or any cohesive social
body. The French words "*esprit de corps*" so vividly ex-

[15] H. B. Sweete, *The Holy Spirit in the Ancient Church*, Macmillan,
1912, page 390. If a further confession of theological ignorance is in
place, here is another from a contemporary theologian: "When we consider the question of the nature and work of God the Holy Ghost, we
find that the Church is without any clearly defined teaching on the
subject, that the doctrine is seldom treated in the pulpit, or in devotional books, and that the notions entertained on the subject by other-
wise well-informed Christians are hazy and confused." From Peter Green,
The Holy Ghost, the Comforter, Longmans, 1933, page 3.

press this corporate fact of observation and experience that
they have become a domesticated phrase. This second use
of the word "spirit" can throw much light on the New Testament story of Pentecost. Of this more later.

Second: The use of both "holy" and "spirit" as applying
to more than one person of the Trinity. God is holy. God
is Spirit. The working of God's "Spirit" cannot be limited
to post-Pentecostal history. Yet "Holy Spirit," as used normally in the New Testament, does mean the gift historically
first imparted at Pentecost. It can at once be admitted that
the distinction between God's holy Spirit and the Pentecostal "Spirit" is not clear in the Bible. Yet a distinction,
nevertheless, is there. To ignore this causes endless confusion.
John Calvin made a shrewd comment on this source of misunderstanding: "When Christ said 'God is Spirit,' He was
uttering the truth that the Divine essence is wholly spiritual,
not using the word Spirit as it is used in other passages, to
mean the third Person hypostatically. Kurios, the New
Testament word for Jehovah, is similarly used sometimes for
Christ and sometimes for the Godhead as a whole." [16] A
modern scholar goes even further and boldly suggests that
the term "Holy Spirit" is really inadequate to describe or
define what the New Testament Church itself meant by it.[17]

With these distinctions in mind, let us turn to the historical
Revelation in the New Testament. One fact looms large.
The prevailing modern identification of the Holy Spirit with
the divine element in man, or with God's immanent working
in man, finds little basis in the scriptural record. Of course,

[16] *Institutes*, Part 1, Chap. 13, sec. 20.
[17] Erich Seeberg, *Christliche Dogmatik*, Leipzig, 1925, vol. 2, page 331:
"*Die Bezeichnung als 'heiliger Geist' ist in der Tat unzulänglich, denn
da Gott und ebenso Christus sowohl Geist als auch heilig, das heist
überweltlich, sind, so drückt sie nicht aus, worin die Besonderheit des
heiligen Geistes eigentlich bestehe.*"

God does work thus. There is a light "which lighteth every man that cometh into the world" (John 1:9). There is a law of God universally known, even among the heathen, and "written in their hearts, their conscience also bearing witness, and their thoughts the meanwhile accusing or else excusing one another" (Rom. 2:15). To ascribe such immanent, psychological, universal activity of the divine to "Holy Spirit" is almost inevitable when we think of religion philosophically. But, despite a few possible exceptions, such immanentism is simply not Biblical. One of the most recent surveys of the occurrence of the word Spirit (Ruach) even in the Old Testament concludes: "The original associations of the word *Ruach* are with a definitely supernatural energy, not with anything natural or purely human. In connection with God, the word *Ruach* always suggests energetic action rather than immanance. It represents an invasive, rather than pervasive power." In the New Testament "there is no teaching about the Spirit of God except in direct connexion with the life and work of the Messiah Jesus." [18] The Holy Spirit is mentioned in connection with the conception and baptism of Jesus, as having foretold Him in the prophets—and then as the Pentecostal event. Bishop Gore, whose book, *The Holy Spirit and the Church*, is perhaps the clearest treatment of the whole Biblical view says: "If the New Testament does not *exclude* the idea of the universal operation of the Holy Spirit of which we get a glimpse in the Old Testament, it says nothing about it." "When all is said and acknowledged, there remains a difference, so great as to be startling, between the popular modern view and that of the New Testament." [19]

[18] O. C. Quick, *The Doctrines of the Creeds*, Scribner, 1938, pages 275–276.
[19] *The Holy Spirit and the Church*, Scribner, 1924, pages 19–20.

From the point of view of a doctrine of the Church, two things are exceptionally striking in the event of Pentecost and the descent of the Holy Spirit upon the Fellowship in the upper room.

First: The Holy Spirit is henceforth a corporate, not an individual, possession. Church and Holy Spirit are from this point on inseparable. The Church is called by St. Paul the Body of Christ. The word Body means, again, a community. St. Paul may, indeed, have invented this corporate meaning for the word. The Spirit dwells in the Body. Apart from this corporate community, there is no gift of the Holy Spirit. Hence the importance of baptism—as of the sacraments generally. Baptism is the rite of entrance to the new society of the Spirit. The unbelievable has happened. That which is holy has become "common." In Greek, as partly in English, "common" was used in contrast to "holy." "In the Old Testament the notion of the holiness which is the essential characteristic of God excludes the notion of a common sharing." [20] The new society, however, is precisely the "commonalty" or fellowship of the Holy Spirit, in which the Spirit is both creative agent and a shared gift.

Prophecy, once limited to special messengers of God, is now the possession of all. To a Hebrew, this seemed a miracle—a fulfillment of the prediction of Joel that God in the last days would pour out His Spirit "upon all flesh." But prophecy was not to be tried by the individual apart from the group (2 Cor. 14). The Spirit was a possession of the Body. Hence the importance of remaining One Body. A great wonder at the utter miracle of the Church as possessor of the Pentecostal gift runs through the writings of the early Church. The First Epistle of St. Peter suggests that

[20] O. C. Quick, *The Doctrines of the Creeds,* page 284.

even the angels look upon the Church with envy (1 Peter 1:12).

Did an individual possess the Spirit? Yes, but only if he shared the life of the community. The degree to which an individual partook of "spiritual" gifts was commensurate with the degree to which he shared in the corporate disciplines of brotherhood. An early Christian document pleads: "When thou teachest command and remind the people that they be constant in the assembly of the Church; so that ye be not hindered and make smaller by a member the Body of Christ. . . . Do not deprive our Saviour of His members; do not mangle and scatter His Body." [21] Wrong-doing within the Brotherhood is sin against the Holy Spirit. The sin of Ananias and Sapphira (Acts 5:1–11) can be understood only in the light of this high doctrine of the Church. Many lies were told in Jerusalem on that same day, which went unpunished with death. Ananias and Sapphira had lied to the Fellowship of the Spirit!

Applications of this historic picture of Holy Spirit and Church to later Church life crowd upon the imagination. The New Testament Church, taken as a norm, can stand in judgment over whole areas of mistaken later developments. What, in the light of the common life in the Body of Christ, should be said of individualistic piety (Catholic and Protestant), of the mystical flight of the "alone to the alone," of prayer when it is not related to "Common Prayer," of sacraments which have lost their corporate meaning and merge with magic, of sacerdotalism which monopolizes spiritual powers belonging to the Church as a whole?

To think of "spirit" or "spiritual" with a social meaning

[21] *Didascalia*, chap. 13. Quoted by W. J. Phythian-Adams in *Church Quarterly Review*, June, 1943.

is strange to most modern religious thought. To reintroduce us to such a social meaning of the word "spirit," I venture to employ an analogy. It has already been referred to—the analogy of the corporate "spirit" of a school or college, or an *"esprit de corps."*

We have all experienced such "spirit." At a football game the spirit of a college produces phenomena not so different from those related of Pentecost. A whole stadium full of people can be brought to its feet, as if by the rush of a mighty wind, when the corporate spirit moves. I have known sedate professors who "spoke with tongues," uttering words they later disavowed. Spirit in this social sense means power. It gives to an individual transcendence over himself. Many a football game has been won by the spirit of a school.

The analogy applies further. How can *"esprit de corps"* be acquired? Certainly not by mere hard work or even by a man's making himself worthy of it. It comes by "grace." He must be accepted as a member of the Body which has the spirit. Then the spirit is his for the asking. In other words, the gift of *"esprit de corps"* comes by way of an initiation sacrament of some sort. Take the Yale spirit, as a concrete example. A stranger to Yale, living at a distance, might make himself master of its history and might achieve a code of conduct on the best Yale models. All this would not make him a Yale man. An ignorant and irresponsible freshman, actually enrolled in the university, would possess more of the Yale spirit than any outsider, however deserving. *"Esprit de corps"* is a social possession. It must be imparted. It cannot be earned. No individual, as such, can own it. It is "spirit." It is also tied to "body." It cannot be "spiritually" acquired. If possession of an *"esprit de corps"* is thought of in terms of some form of salvation, the doctrine *extra ecclesiam nulla salus* can find easy analogies in all corporate life—no "salvation" outside the concrete corporate body which alone can impart the saving spirit. The absolute necessity of sacraments can find equally striking analogies, and the analogies, in turn, can explain what is wrong with sacramentalism when it has lost its social reference. "*Esprit de corps*" simply lives on sacramental "grace."

Now it may be granted at once that the analogy is not perfect. It breaks down when the origin of "*esprit de corps*" is brought into the picture. A human social group can, in a way, create "*esprit de corps*," though the origin of a corporate "spirit" always involves a mystery. The Christian community did not create the Holy Spirit. God the Holy Spirit founded the community. Furthermore, entrance to the Christian community involved a confession of faith as well as baptism. A oneness of belief was essential. Faith stood guard over "spirits." Faith was a test of "spirits." Many of these essential elements in the picture of the New Testament Church cannot find exact parallels in the secular scene. The analogy is only analogy.

Yet the analogy, critically used, can illuminate the doctrine of the Holy Spirit of the New Testament and can shed light on many puzzles of Church life in our own day. I pause here for only one example—the problem of prayer.

Let us take, as a concrete point of departure, the remarkable verse on prayer in St. Paul's Epistle to the Romans (8:26): "Likewise the Spirit also helpeth our infirmities: for we know not what we should pray for as we ought: but the Spirit itself maketh intercession for us." Read this with the individualistic, modern interpretation of the Holy Spirit in mind, and the verse has, of course, meaning. But read it with the corporate Spirit in mind, and it has meaning also, and can place a guard upon selfish prayer. For Spirit, substitute Fellowship of the Holy Spirit. "The Fellowship also helpeth our infirmities: for we (apart from the Fellowship of the Holy Spirit) know not what we should pray for as we ought." . . . Normal Christian prayer is Church prayer, common prayer. "If two of you shall agree on earth as touching any thing that they shall ask, it shall be done for them of my Father which is in heaven." For when two are gathered, the miracle of the divine Presence happens. The Church is there; the Spirit is there. And the Spirit is God Himself. "For where two or three are gathered together in my name, there am I in the midst of them" (Matt. 18:19, 20). *Ubi tres, ibi ecclesia.*

To accept such a view of prayer is not easy for a Christianity brought up on individualistic Protestant piety or equally individualistic Catholic mysticism. The tradition of the mystical prayer life of the Counter-Reformation (now almost universally accepted as normative in teaching prayer) can be subjected to severe critical judgment in the light of the Biblical doctrine of the Spirit and of the Church. I am prepared to voice my own conviction that it has been a danger for the Church—as the Liturgical Movement within Rome itself is beginning to say openly. Any individualistic flight of the "alone to the alone," any escape from corporate historic living, finds scant support in the New Testament. Christian mysticism comes late in Christian history because the New Testament sense of corporate life in the Body of Christ was still too powerful. This older anchorage of the prayer life of Christians in the Fellowship can be seen in a quotation from the Reformation figure, Richard Hooker, who almost warns against individualist prayer altogether: "When we publicly make our prayers, it cannot be but that we do it with much more comfort than in private, for that the things we ask publicly are approved as needful and good in the judgment of all, we hear them sought for and desired with common consent. 'For even prayer itself,' saith St. Basil, 'when it hath not the consort of many voices to strengthen it, is not itself.' " [22]

Of course, such a doctrine of prayer does not rule out prayer "in the closet," any more than the gift of the Holy Spirit can be refused to the individual. Frederick Denison Maurice, in his eloquent defense of Church prayer, resolves the tension between corporate and individual prayer by an appeal to Christ's own teaching: "Not how the selfishness of the closet may be carried into the temple, but how the breadth and universality which belong to the temple may be attained in the closet. When thou art most alone, thou must still, if thou wouldest pray, be in the midst of a family; thou must call upon a Father; thou must not dare to say *my*, but *our*." [23]

I refrain from further applications of the doctrine of the corporate Holy Spirit to Church life today. Such applications could revolutionize many of our "spiritual" disciplines and much of our ecclesiastical machinery. "*Ecclesiastical*," says Bishop Gore, "ought to mean *brotherly*. It did really mean this in the days when it cost men much to call themselves Christians. If the first Christians had not been bound together by the necessity of adherence to the one Church and its sacraments and ministry—if they had not identified salvation with membership in the one divine society represented by the local Church—the disruptive tendencies of class and race and tradition would have rendered the divine attempt to establish a catholic fellowship nugatory from the beginning. Here we get the fundamental reason why *credo in sanctam catholicam ecclesiam* follows at once on *credo in Spiritum Sanctum*. How to make the principle of this

[22] Richard Hooker, *Ecclesiastical Polity* 5.24.2.
[23] F. D. Maurice, *The Kingdom of Christ*, Everyman Edition, 2.26.

sequence effective again in modern society is, I think, actually the most important matter for consideration by Christians of the present day." [24]

Ascension and Pentecost

I turn now to a second comment on the importance of the Pentecostal event for a doctrine of the Church.

The Ascension and Pentecost were accepted by the early Church as marking a profound change in relationship between the original disciple group and the Jesus of the Gospel story. This change has, I think, not always been fully realized in later Church attitudes toward Christ. Whatever may have been the actual events underlying the Ascension story, that event brought to a definite close the ministry of Christ "in the flesh." Even further Resurrection experiences were no longer expected. Jesus was now no longer present on the human plane. He was now the Lord, ascended, and glorified. This time-sequence of events was vividly apprehended and never forgotten. Past and present were not confused. Jesus had once been a baby in his mother's arms. But He was not that *now*. He had once been Rabbi, Master, Teacher, Friend. But He was not that *now*. God had now "set him at His own right hand in the heavenly places . . . and hath put all things under His feet, and gave Him to be head over all things to the Church, which is His body" (Eph. 1:20–23). He was expected to return, but not as the Jesus of the Gospel story. He would return as Judge. Indeed, the picture of Christ as Judge was very vivid to the New Testament Church.[25] He appears frequently as Judge

[24] Charles Gore, *The Holy Spirit and the Church*, Scribner, 1924, page 28.
[25] See H. L. Goudge, *The Apocalypse and the Present Age*, Mowbray, 1935, page 25.

in the Revelation of St. John, but also in St. Paul: "For we must all appear before the judgment seat of Christ. . . . Knowing therefore the terror of the Lord, we persuade men" (2 Cor. 5:10, 11).

Hence all relationship with Christ, subsequent to the Ascension, was radically different from the disciple-master relationship which had been normal during His earthly life. The Second Person of the Trinity was *now* no longer on the historical scene. The Third Person had taken His place. Christ remained as pattern and as founder of the New Covenant. But the "Covenant in His blood" and the Spirit as Presence were the great legacies of the Jesus of the Gospel drama. It was the *work* of Christ, not first of all His historical person, which was a present appropriation. One wonders what the early Church would have said of the Jesus-piety of mediaeval and modern Christianity. No sentimental hymns to Jesus occur in the New Testament.

The contrast between early and later Christian attitudes toward the Jesus of history can be sharply seen in such a matter as discipleship. In our contemporary Christianity this is one of our most familiar words. We intend by it, I presume, a recreation of the master-follower relationship. The content of the covenant relationship with Christ (if the word covenant applies at all) is ethical imitation. But is such a relationship any longer possible? Jesus is expected to enter somehow into our time as a man like ourselves. He was "very man" once. The New Testament Church wrote the Gospels in which this story of incarnation is told and upon which its Faith in the Redeemer rested. Yet that time can never return. One of the key-texts of the New Testament is St. Paul's saying: "Though we have known Christ after the flesh, yet now henceforth know we him no more" (2 Cor. 5:16). What, indeed, can the Jesus of human history now do for us?

We need a present Saviour, not a model or an example or teacher out of the past. The early Church rightly preached the Cross and the Resurrection and the gift of the Spirit. These are the positive gospel which alone makes Christians. We can appropriate these. They are the work of Christ, ushering us into the new relationship with Himself and the Father. As P. T. Forsyth says: "Churches are not made of disciples (who turned traitors), but of those who had gone through what made them apostles, confessors, martyrs." [26] It is indeed remarkable how the years spent by the disciples in the company of the Master produced so disappointing a result. But the event of Pentecost transformed them. The word "disciple" does not occur in the New Testament after the Acts of the Apostles and even in that book the word describes the historic apostolic band of witnesses and is not a generic term for Christians. There is, of course, a truth in the modern twist of the Christian life into discipleship. The Christ of history is not to be confused with Christ as Spirit. The Second Person of the Trinity must remain always Pattern and Judge. That is what the figures "Head of the Church" and "Bridegroom of the Church" partly mean. Christ and Holy Spirit almost merge in certain New Testament passages, notably 2 Cor. 3:17. The point is, however, that Christ's presence is no longer as Second Person. The Church now is indwelt by the Third Person, the Holy Spirit. Was it not this vivid experience in the early Church of an end to the master-disciple relationship and the beginning of a new era of the Holy Spirit which alone can explain Trinitarian doctrine? Has later Christianity (mediaeval and modern), though it paid lip service to Trinitarian formulae, really believed in the Third Person?

[26] P. T. Forsyth, *The Church and the Sacraments*, Longmans, 1917, page 20.

The gulf which separates discipleship-Christianity and covenant-Christianity is so great that one is almost baffled to describe it. A gulf also exists between Church Christianity of the New Testament and the Jesus mysticism of later development.

> Jesus, Lover of my soul,
> Let me to Thy bosom fly.

One hesitates to lay violent hands on a hymn which is still the soul-food of millions. Yet would not the New Testament Church have been a little shocked by such words? Jesus had become the Christ in glory. "From thence he shall come to judge the quick and the dead." His coming, indeed, was momentarily expected. He was Lord. To come into His presence sitting at the right hand of God, was not to be thought of without awesome preparation. He had wrought salvation through His mighty acts. The Christian through Him could have access to the holy God. But He was not now the Comforter. "Another Comforter" had come (John 15:26).

Can we not fall back in this matter upon the age-long experience of Christians, regardless of how faultily we express ourselves in our hymns and our theology? We become conscious (and this is already grace) of the gulf between human guilt and God's holy law. We hear the Gospel, the good news that holy law is also holy love. We hear the story of God's revealing His love in the mighty acts of Redemption. A new relationship (covenant) is made possible for us through what Christ has done. He has opened the way for a sinner to come into the presence of the holy God. Has this miracle happened through personal contact, across the centuries, with the Jesus of Jerusalem and Galilee? How is such a relationship realistically possible? Through nostalgic memory? Has not the miracle in us been wrought first of all by the work of Christ, rather than by His person? Of course, the person stands behind the mighty objective act of Atonement. The Jesus of history is *now* "at the right hand of the Father" and reconciliation with the Father means personal relationship with Christ also. But the relationship is precisely with the risen glorified Christ. We must approach even Him through the redemptive covenant which He has bequeathed to us. And that covenant is historically alive in the Fellowship. The Fellowship takes me, a sinner, and gives me the status of "a child of God and an inheritor of the Kingdom of heaven." The Fellowship exercises divine powers. The Fellowship forgives sins. It is the society of the forgiven and the forgiving. It is the society of *agape*. This Christian love is not of human creation. It is grace. The early Church saw its divine character so clearly that it recognized this power as a person—God the Holy Spirit.

P. T. Forsyth, in his great book on the Church (one of the wisest written in modern times) [27] dwells on this importance of Christ's redemptive work in contrast to his appeal as "Master" repeatedly. "What is it in Him," he asks, "that makes Him head? What is it in the nature of His headship that makes His company a real society, His society a real Kingdom and His historic following a Church? Is He but the chief of a clan He inherits, the center of a group He attracts; or is He King of a realm He creates? Are we but disciples of His person or are we confessors of His redemption?" [28] Or again: "Our communion is . . . not with His person except as that person in its consummate and eternal Act is our Redeemer. It is not the spell of that person that we own, but its saving grace that we worship. We do not

[27] P. T. Forsyth, *The Church and the Sacraments*, Longmans, 1917.
[28] *Ibid.*, pages 53–54.

enjoy its kind beauty, nor drink up its sympathy, but live on its act and power." [29]

Having, however, said all this as a corrective to sentimental "personal religion," let me add a word on the other side. The work of Christ does come first. We cannot approach the holy God except through the Cross. We never outgrow the need for justification before God and before the Christ of glory and judgment. Yet within the covenant of reconciliation, the way is open for the warmth of personal nearness and companionship with the Ascended Lord who yet took with Him to the "heavenlies" the very manhood of His incarnate life. We can "come boldly unto the throne of grace" (Heb. 5:16). Personal commitment can assume its rightful place in Christian life. Yet personal commitment cannot be (and here lies the danger of "personal religion") a substitute for reconciliation through the Cross. Personal relationship with Christ, as with the Father, is a gift and a reward. It cannot take the place of the objective work of Christ—the Atonement. The risen Christ remains Lord.

The classic prayers of the Christian Church are addressed *to* the Father, *through* the Son, *in* the Fellowship of the Holy Spirit. This formula epitomizes Christian experience of God's grace. The center of Christian Faith is still the holy God Himself. Christ is Mediator. The Spirit in the Church is present. To substitute for this approach to the holy God a non-historical, sentimental relationship with Christ in the flesh is unrealistic. Individualistic Christianity has suffered from such sentimentalism for centuries. A. E. Taylor, commenting on the futility of this Jesus cult, particularly in its ethical form, goes so far as to say: "One may fairly doubt whether any man has ever really been converted to the

[29] *Ibid.*, page 284.

Christian faith simply by the impression made on him either by the story of Christ's life or by the reports of His moral teaching." The early Christians, so A. E. Taylor asserts in the same connection, believed in the Lordship of Christ "because they were first convinced that they had in themselves the actual experience of a new kind of life with God as its center, and that this life had begun with the Pentecostal 'giving of the Spirit.' They did not infer the transcendent significance of Christ from an antecedent belief in the moral perfection of his character, or the ethical elevation of his recorded sayings: rather they inferred these—though it is singular how little appeal any of the New Testament writers outside the Synoptic Gospels make to ethical precepts of Jesus—from their antecedent belief in the transcendent significance of Christ as the 'glorified' sender of the Spirit." [30] If such an interpretation of the sequence of God's mighty acts in His drama of salvation were once again fully grasped by Christian thought, a revolution would be in order in whole areas of Christian education and preaching.

The amazing power of the early Church to convert the pagan Roman world was based upon its positive Gospel of Redemption, but equally upon itself. For the power of the corporate Spirit of the redeemed in Christ is incalculable. The slave is made equal with the master. Burdens are shared in Christian love. The sick are healed by the laying on of hands of the loving brotherhood. Demons of loneliness and fear are driven out. Down through the centuries this power of the Spirit, "proceeding from the Father and the Son," has fed Christian life. It made possible even pietistic individualism. Has this, in fact, ever appeared except in a rich soil of

[30] A. E. Taylor, *The Faith of a Moralist*, Macmillan, 1932, vol. 2, page 130.

evangelical community life, nurtured in cottage prayer meeting or in the Christian family, which has well been called "a little Church"? Individualistic Christianity is, at bottom, an illusion. Its chief error lies in its being blind to the source of its own "spiritual" power. For this is still the Gospel in the Family of God.

Dom Anscar Vonier, a leader in the Liturgical Movement in the Roman Church, puts the contrast between the New Testament apprehension of the Holy Spirit in the Church and later misunderstandings thus: "We are inclined to establish this difference between the coming of Christ and the coming of the Spirit, that the first is manifest whilst the second is hidden. Such is not original Christian thinking. According to apostolic language, it is Christ who hides after He accomplished His work here on earth and it is the Spirit who is made manifest. The Spirit is the true theophany after Christ's ascension till the Lord returns again from heaven in the glory of the Father." [31] This is the paradox of a truly "high" Church doctrine. The Church of God will not come into its own until it is seen once more as the mightiest of the mighty acts of God.

The "Colony of Heaven"

The "mystery of the Fellowship," to use St. Paul's phrase, is not, of course, exhausted by disclosing the intimate connection between Church and Holy Spirit. The New Testament literally is studded with insights and figures of speech regarding the Church, each of which beckons to exploration. Only a few can be so much as mentioned in this place. St.

[31] Vonier, Dom Anscar, *The Spirit and the Bride*, Burns Oates, 1935, page 14.

Paul speaks of the Church as the "household of faith"—a family metaphor.[32] The Church is "Jerusalem which is above . . . which is the mother of us all" (Gal. 4:26). The Church is "the temple of God" (I Cor. 3:16). More frequently and more importantly, the Church is both the Body and the Bride of Christ. The two figures are interwoven in the great passage on marriage of Ephesians 5:22 ff. The Church as Bride may, indeed, be the more original, from which the figure of the Church as Body is taken. The Old Testament could furnish St. Paul with many parallels in the use of this nuptial analogy.

The Church as Bride is an important metaphor. It can serve as a check upon the Church's presuming upon her rights. For the Bride, as St. Paul and the Old Testament analogues clearly portray her, is subject to the Bridegroom. "For the Husband is the head of the wife, even as Christ is the head of the Church" (Eph. 5:23). Christ as Judge enters thus once more into the picture. The Church is holy. The Church however, does not thereby escape judgment. This paradox runs through the New Testament as the Old. It can be an eternal warning to the churches of later history. To this truth the Reformation made justified appeal in its break with Rome.[33]

The paradox portrayed in the fact that the Church is both holy and yet sinful helps to solve, too, the vexed question of

[32] Gal. 6:10. Compare "The whole family in heaven and earth" of Eph. 3:15.
[33] See Claude Chavasse, *The Bride of Christ,* The Religious Book Club, 1941. This study of the doctrine of the Church is very helpful. It appeals to the New Testament against later loss of the corporate idea of the Church. Nowhere can this loss of the doctrine of the Church be more clearly seen than in the individualistic twist given to the Bride-Bridegroom relationship in mediaeval Catholic piety—from which Protestant piety drew much of its meaning. In the Middle Ages, the nun, or the solitary Christian soul, became the Bride of Christ.

the relation of the Church to the Kingdom of God of Jesus' own teaching. Clearly, the connection is close. Yet Church cannot be Kingdom. The Church is the Kingdom "in the making." It is the Kingdom in history. It is the corporate sacrament of the Kingdom. It is, as Karl Barth puts it, "the Kingdom between the times"—between the Lord's first and His second coming. F. D. Maurice calls the Church "The Kingdom of Christ" (in the classic book by that name). Better still the Church might be called "The Kingdom of the Holy Spirit." The danger of pride and of attempted escape from judgment always has beset the historic Church. This danger is clearly seen in the phrase so often used by Catholic writers, defining the Church as "the extension of the Incarnation." The phrase is unscriptural. Guardedly used, it contains a truth. But the Catholic tradition has sinned precisely in using it unguardedly. One of the issues causing the Reformation can be traced to Rome's equating of a sinful, historic Church with the Head of the Church—Incarnate God Himself. The scriptural figures for the Church—Bride of Christ, Body of Christ—are very much safer.

Little enough, too, can here be said of the Church's relation to the world. A remarkable insight, however, into this puzzling tension between the Church and the human society in which the Church lives her life is offered in one other New Testament figure of speech not yet mentioned. This figure may prove to be a light on our path as we wrestle out a doctrine of the Church in the midst of our era of revolutions, when the "World" is assuming corporate, demonic forms. It is a pity that the English translation in the Authorized Version of this saying of St. Paul (Phil. 3:20) has obscured its vivid meaning. The Authorized Version has it, speaking of Christians in the midst of earthly temptations: "Our conversation is in heaven." The Revised Version improves upon this: "Our citizenship is in heaven." The Greek word is *politeuma*, meaning a commonwealth. Luther's German translation has it: *"Unser Wandel ist im Himmel"* — our "wayfaring" is in heaven. But Moffatt's *New Translation* gives the inspired rendering: "We are a colony of heaven."

The Church is a colony of heaven! Here is tension and resolution in a word. Think of a Roman colony, in St. Paul's day, in an alien barbarian land. Roman citizenship would be a treasured possession. Roman culture would be preserved and guarded and handed down from father to son. No individual, however, would be able to keep the tradition of the homeland alive by himself. He would seek the support of his fellows in exile. Corporate nurture alone would serve. For the colony was both memory and foretaste of home. Members of the colony would be compelled to deal with outsiders. The colony might indeed have been planted as a missionary enterprise—imperial Rome winning loyalty for her great *Pax Romana*. Tension would exist, and compromise. Roman citizen and barbarian neighbor might be outwardly scarcely distinguishable. Yet what a difference in ultimate loyalties, in heart's longing, or in memories.

Is not this the life of the people of God in the World? We, too, are only a colony of heaven. We are not the homeland of the final Communion of Saints, but even less are we the alien world which has not been won to membership in the Family of Christ. Our life is tension, and even compromise. To escape from tension is a denial of our mission in historic existence. The ascetic escapist avoids the tension by withdrawing into memory or mystic contemplation of home. The secularist, on the other extreme, exchanges his heavenly citizenship for one in the world. Neither is fulfilling his difficult but glorious vocation as a member of the colony of heaven.

For the Church of God is the Kingdom after Pentecost but before the Final Judgment. It is the Kingdom *in history*. It has a missionary task to perform. It is the dragnet of Jesus' own parable, gathering "of every kind." For centuries the mission of the Church has been partially obscured. The colony had lived so long in the alien country that the difference between the two had been forgotten. Professional missionaries, sent into obviously heathen lands, alone kept fully alive the Church's sense of her vocation. Citizenship in heaven was no longer valued as a treasure of great price. But the days of ease are over. The Church is no longer a "spiritual" Body without rivals. Spirits other than the Holy Spirit are ruling in giant corporate incarnations once more. The Body of Christ is not the only Body which can have "Spirit." There may be a Body of Satan, with powers so manifest that they rival those of Pentecost and perform mighty works. These rival demonic Churches may win converts by the millions.

Citizenship in the commonwealth of the people of God will, however, become precious in its turn also. All over the Christian world, lonely Christian souls will discover that they are members of the Body of Christ, members one of another. Christian love, that revelation of the divine in the corporate life of the Fellowship, will become manifest once more across the hedges and walls of ecclesiasticisms. The Christian flocks since the Reformation have been a nation "scattered and peeled" (Isaiah 18:2). But "He that scattered Israel will gather him, as a shepherd doth his flock. . . . Therefore they shall come and sing in the height of Zion and shall flow together to the goodness of the Lord.

. . . That they might be unto me for a people, and for a
name, and for a praise, and for a glory, saith the Lord"
(Jer. 31:10, 12; 13:11).

ADDITIONAL NOTE

The critical student of the New Testament may question
whether the word *pneuma* can be limited as applying to a corporate spirit. I should say at once that it cannot thus be limited.
Neither was the word *soma*, body, restricted to corporate use.
Yet both words do receive such social interpretation. When
the author of Ephesians says (4:4): "There is one body, and
one Spirit," he is undoubtedly referring to Holy Spirit as a
corporate possession. And this verse is typical.

I have, I admit, never seen the analogy of *"esprit de corps"*
applied to the New Testament doctrine of the Holy Spirit. The
nearest equivalent I have met is in Schleiermacher's *Der Christliche Glaube*.[34] Schleiermacher speaks of the Holy Spirit as
the *Gemeingeist* of the Christian community—"the collective
spirit which animates the communal life of believers."

A friend of mine cites a sentence of Alexander Vinet as a
parallel: *"L'Esprit Sainte est Dieu Social."* I have, however,
failed, despite considerable research, to locate the reference. The
sentence is startling and suggestive.

Frederick Denison Maurice expresses a corporate view of the
doctrine of the Holy Spirit as follows: "Without a covenant
we are not members of a Body; the Spirit dwells in the Body,
and in each of its members *as such*, and not as individuals. The
Spirit in an individual is a fearful contradiction." [35]

On the "Spirit" as a divine power in the corporate Church,
E. G. Selwyn [36] has an illuminating discussion. He employs the
following analogy: "The Totem-cults and initiations and tabus
which abound in the tribal lore of primeval or still savage man;

[34] Sec. ed., Berlin, 1836, vol. 2, page 293.
[35] *Life of Maurice*, by J. E. Maurice, Scribner, 1884, vol. 1, page 209.
[36] *The Approach to Christianity*, Longmans, 1925, page 210.

the *pietas* which surrounded the Lares and Penates of the Roman family; the solemn ritual with which the Greek celebrated the patron god or goddess of his *polis*, or inaugurated the pan-Hellenic games at Nemea or Olympus—all these attest the conviction that there was something 'numinous' in the functioning of the great social institutions of humanity."

III

THE CATHOLIC-PROTESTANT CHASM

Almost any Anglican, if asked to express his critical appraisal of the ecumenical discussions of our generation, would be compelled to lament one major omission in the usual agenda. The ecumenical movement has as yet not fully and frankly faced the challenge of historic Catholicism. This is a broad generalization which deserves much modification. The Catholic view of the episcopate and of the ministry has received fair attention and is acknowledged as one of the chief bars to easy reunion schemes. The sacraments have been viewed from Catholic as well as Protestant points of view and the same comprehension of discussion has touched many other topics. Yet most Anglicans would still insist that the real debate on ultimate problems of Church reunion has only just begun—if such reunion is going to include any Catholic-minded Church bodies at all.

It is a puzzling fact, for example, that the doctrine of the Church has received comparatively little attention in ecumenical conferences dealing with Faith and Order. The late Archbishop of Canterbury (then Archbishop of York) called attention to this omission in his opening address to the Edinburgh Conference. Representatives of Eastern Orthodoxy and of the Anglo-Catholic wing of Anglicanism have participated fully in the ecumenical conferences of the past generation and their views have, of course, had a hearing. I would not accuse Protestant churchmen of ignorance or obscurantism. But would not many of these Protestant spokesmen themselves admit that the Catholic-Protestant chasm does not really loom large as yet in their ecumenical theology, and that the building of bridges across this major historic schism is still, for the most part, outside their ecumenical dreams? The South India Union Scheme involves at least one such bridge. But debate on this scheme has been far more voluble on the Catholic than on the Protestant side.

Now it is possible that the major ecumenical developments of the future may take place in Protestant Church life alone and will leave even Anglo-Catholicism, or Anglicanism itself, on one side. I doubt that this can happen. But even if it did happen, the day of reckoning with the Catholic-Protestant chasm in Christendom could only be postponed. The Roman Church may never, in reasonably conceived historic time, join the ecumenical movement. But there is Eastern Orthodoxy and there is Anglicanism. Above all, there is the Catholic idea of the Church itself. "Ecumenical" may be a valuable synonym for "Catholic," freed, for a time, from some of the embarrassing ambiguities which encumber the traditional adjective for the Church in the creeds. But, from the point of view of the Christian Faith, it means the same thing. Wrestle long enough with the *idea* of an ecumenical Church, and the embodiments of that idea in the historic Catholicisms of Church history must, sooner or later, be dealt with also. There is, in this world, no complete emancipation from history.

I would plead, accordingly, for granting to historic Catholicism (including that of Rome) the fullest kind of a hearing in ecumenical debate. This ought to happen before ecumenical movements receive premature crystallizations. If God is setting our feet upon the path toward a reunited

Christendom, surely He is asking us, as we open our hearts and our imaginations to this new dawn, to include consideration of the Catholic Communion of Saints as well as of the Christian fellowships since the Reformation. Such a time of Church reconstruction and rebirth may never come again. Mere historic prejudice, at least, should be laid aside.

I would not be misunderstood, however, as predicting that the ecumenical movement will mean a return to the mediaeval authoritarian Church which Catholicism still connotes. Though I shall treat the Catholic-Protestant chasm in Christendom from an Anglican point of view, sympathetic to Catholic traditions, I shall be compelled to do so from a definite vantage point even within Anglicanism. I join my Protestant brethren in the belief that the Reformation is still the greatest recovery of the Gospel in Christian history since the New Testament itself. If this Gospel should be endangered by sympathetic consideration of the Church life on the other side of the chasm, we had best leave historic Catholicism strictly alone. This fear, I suspect, animates much of the hesitation of evangelical thought. Anglicanism itself once made the great decision to join the Protestant revolt against mediaeval Rome. All attempts to break the ties of Anglicanism with the Reformation Churches have been, I am persuaded, something of a denial of the vocation of Anglicanism. The Oxford Movement has taught Anglicanism much. It has revived, for large circles of Protestantism even outside the Anglican Churches, the very idea of the Church as basic to the Christian Gospel. But when it has tried to embody this idea in a return to mediaeval authoritarianism or in sentimental borrowings from Counter-Reformation Rome, it has, I hold, been untrue to some of the most precious things in traditional Anglican Church life. Classical Anglicanism is, on its doctrinal side, evangelical. It is Protestant in the main tendency of its confessional theology, as I think any student of the Thirty-nine Articles would admit. The bridge which classical Anglicanism built across the Catholic-Protestant chasm of the sixteenth century was in the areas of liturgical worship and Church order. It is in these areas that bridges can be built over the same chasm today. The debates within Anglicanism are complicated by the fact that the Catholic elements within it can be treated either as of secondary or of primary importance. They can be accepted as pragmatic, functional forms of the Gospel in history, or as themselves part of the deposit of faith. The latter view is, as I shall argue later, Rome's great error.

The fact remains, however, that Anglicanism has preserved Catholic elements within its Church life through all of its history—whatever doctrinal interpretations have been placed upon them by parties or by individuals. One party will read the story as if Anglicanism had retained Catholic forms by divine providence and 'Reformation theology merely by divine inadvertence. Other parties will read the story with the reverse evaluation. But either way, Catholic elements are there. If the ecumenical movement comes to the point where historic Catholic Christianity is to be seriously considered, Anglicanism can play a mediatorial role. It has gone through the Reformation revolt with Protestantism. It can interpret across the chasm as even Eastern Orthodoxy cannot do.

It will not be easy for the ecumenical movement to include historic Catholicism fully in its purview. Any Anglican can testify to the agony of mediation. Anglicans have lived over the Catholic-Protestant chasm for four hundred years. They have endured the tensions involved in such a conflicting anchorage of historic loyalties. One may express doubt as to whether the tensions have been altogether for good. Resolution of the tension in a larger ecumenical context ought to be welcome. The word "churchmanship," for example, which Anglicans freely bandy about, has become almost grotesquely trivial in its meaning. "Churchmanship," for New Testament Christianity, would have meant "brotherliness." It would have connoted the glorious privileges of membership in the Body of Christ, a willingness to bear one another's burdens, an eagerness to protect tender consciences. With Anglicans, it has become a word of strife. Every parish, almost every member of the clergy, is graded according to a scale of external differences in ceremonial or practice, or even vocabulary. Often these differences concern merely "the little problems of the sanctuary"—matters of stoles or tippets, genuflections, the number of candles on the altar, the use of "Father" or "Mr." for the rector, the word "Mass" or "Holy Communion," detailed disciplines of fasting, and a hundred more. To an outsider, Anglican Church life must at times appear almost ludicrous in the emphasis it seems to place on ecclesiastical externals. No other Christian communion exhibits anything comparable.

Nevertheless, behind this debate on symbols stand great issues. The Anglican evangelical is at one with his Anglo-Catholic brother in the conviction that the historic Catholic tradition has to be reckoned with in any complete conception of the Christian Church. Anglicanism, be it by historic accident or by the ruling of divine Providence, carried over at the Reformation at least some precious values out of the thousand years of Christian life preceding the great revolt. Let the ecumenical movement criticize this Catholic tradition. Let it sharpen the chasm between Rome and Protestantism on certain basic Christian doctrines if it must. But let historic Catholic Church life have a hearing. And, surely, Protestantism can, in our time, assume an attitude of generosity. The "Liberalism" of the nineteenth century has smashed some of Protestantism's own pride. The atomistic Fundamentalisms of the hundreds of Reformation sects can yield to ecumenical criticism. The post-Protestant era of the coming Great Church should be one in which all Christians can, if they will, have a share. Anglicanism has stood guard over certain Catholic insights. It cannot deny this vocation. That may be the burden God has placed upon it. Having guarded its trust, it ought to ask for nothing more, however, than permission to account for that trust before Christ's universal Church. Its own danger may consist in a refusal to submit this trust to ecumenical judgment.

The Chasm

The Catholic-Protestant chasm—how can it be ultimately defined or described?

In the light of a Biblical doctrine of the Church, one generalisation seems to be warranted. The Church is the Kingdom of God in history. Protestantism has clearly been an attempt to make the Kingdom central once more in Christian life. The Reformation began as a revolt of the Christian moral conscience against a corrupt mediaeval Church. So profound was the revolt that the individual conscience was apparently given sovereign rights over against the Church. Behind this magnificent defiance lurked the individualism which has beset Protestantism ever since, an individualism which the early Reformers might have been the first to disavow. Conscience does not become Christian conscience in a vacuum. Luther and Calvin spoke from *within* the historic Church. The Reformation inheritance needs to correct some of its theological thinking on this issue. Yet Roman Catholic polemic, when it dismisses evangelical Christianity as purely individualistic, is utterly unfair. Protestants still worship corporately as do Catholics—more so if the Christian congregation should be taken as norm. Protestant doctrines of the Church have never done justice to evangelical experience.

The Protestant revolt has often been defined as one of prophet against priest. Parallels can be rightly traced between this revolt and that of Amos or Isaiah in the Old Testament. Luther began as a prophetic voice within the institutional Church. He was excommunicated. How do excommunicated members of the people of God live? Blueprints for such Church life are not easy to find. The Reformation revolt was in the name of the Kingdom against the "Church-in-History"—a paradox. Kingdom and history cannot really be separated. Yet Protestantism has, in a measure, tried to live the Kingdom-ideal without a vital contact with its life in history. An Orthodox scholar has described Protestant church order as "a romantic, pseudo-historical reconstruction." [1]

Yet Protestantism's subjection of the Church-in-history to the judgment of the Kingdom must be held to be justified. This is what the restitution of the Bible as authority implied. Half of the New Testament doctrine of the Church (the more important half, so many would say) was recovered at the Reformation. When Bible Christianity and Church Christianity are set over against each other, this really endangers a true view. The Reformation, too, was a Church Christianity.

Nevertheless, the Church is the Kingdom *in history*. Attempts to extricate it are bound to prove futile. Sect after sect has tried this. Each denomination, even the most recent,

---

[1] Sergius Boulgakoff, *The Hierarchy and the Sacraments* in *The Ministry and the Sacraments*, ed. Dunkerley, Macmillan, 1937, page 112.

enters history and reduplicates a development into a minor version of Catholicism—the guarding of a succession, the development of a sacramental system, the growth of hierarchical authorities. These Reformation Churches, have, to be sure, preserved the moral earnestness which the Kingdom ideal expresses. What would have happened to Rome itself if the Counter-Reformation had not borrowed spiritual strength from Protestant conscience? This can be seen vividly in countries where Rome has had no Protestant rival. John R. Mott, returning from a tour of South America, reports his sad impression that after four hundred years of undisputed control, the Roman Church had failed to give South America a conscience. Alexander Vinet comments on the whole modern movement: "The Reformation has been the saving of Christianity; without it, not only would Catholicism have failed to purify itself, but have known no arrest in its degeneration; not only is it to the Reformation that the seventeenth century owes Bossuet, Fenelon, Pascal, as it owed to it Abbadie and Saurin; but I would say further, that but for it, Catholicism would no longer exist, because all the branches whatever would have had to perish with the trunk. Rome pretends that there would no longer be Christians if there were no longer Catholics; and we maintain that but for the Reformation there would no longer be Catholics, because there would no longer be Christians." [2]

Few historians would deny that some truth at least is contained in Vinet's boast. The very glory of its achievement, however, might induce Protestantism to admit defeat on one issue. It did not solve the problem of its own life in history. Historical living demands forms and institutions, sacraments, and a Church order. To treat these as ultimately indifferent is simply an illusion. Furthermore, to find these forms in

[2] Alexander Vinet, *Outlines of Theology*, London, 1866, page 418.

Biblical literalism is unhistorical also. Church polity is about the worst place in which to try out Bible Fundamentalism. Is the Church order of any Christian community a true return to the life of the primitive Church? Group after group have tried such false historicism—all different, all slowly encrusting themselves in miniature Catholicisms. Let Protestantism lift Bible and the Gospel of the Holy Kingdom of God to its rightful place as norm of the Church. Let it keep the prophetic protest against ecclesiasticism. Let the Reformation principle be maintained as part of the very essence of Church life. But Protestantism needs desperately to reexamine the means it has used to preserve the Church's conscience. This cannot be done by escaping the relativities of history. Even Quakerism, the most uncompromising experiment of Christianity without institutionalism, is an eloquent testimony of the fact that there is no escape. Church order *is* important. Sacraments are of the essence of corporate historical existence. On this issue historic Catholicism is surely right. Indeed, for fifteen hundred years, from the Church of the New Testament to the Reformation, this truth was rarely so much as questioned.

The Church is the Kingdom in history. If Protestantism recovered the importance of the Kingdom as norm in the Church's ongoing life, Catholicism exhibits the other half of the doctrine. But if Protestantism has erred in onesidedness, Catholicism has erred even more dangerously. It has confused the Kingdom in history with the Kingdom itself. The Church-in-history is absolutized. The institutional embodiment of the Church of Faith herself becomes virtually the Incarnation. We find it difficult to recapture the virulence of sixteenth-century dispute. But when Luther and Calvin thundered against Rome as Antichrist and against "popish idolatry," they had this error of Catholicism in mind. And here the Reformers, in their turn, were right, however much one may wish to soften their vocabulary.

A paradox plainly confronts us in the Catholic-Protestant tension. Each sees part of the truth. To disentangle error from falsehood, to readmit into the Protestant view of the Church insight into the meaning of history and to dethrone historical absolutism in Catholicism—this will require statesmanship of a high order. A challenge confronts the ecumenical theology of the future. Catholicism commits a great error. But it is not all wrong. Catholicism has possessed almost a monopoly of the *idea* of the universal, historic, visible Church. She has stood as massive guardian over an entire millennium of Christian history and experience.

Let us suppose that an observer, with prejudices held in check, visits both a Roman Catholic and an evangelical church and notes contrasts. What will he see?

In a Roman Catholic Church he will confess at once that he is in the presence of mystery. The corporate experience of many centuries has here found symbols. Crosses everywhere, and candles, a central altar reminiscent of religious man from prehistoric time. Here is a great institution before which even the pagan unbeliever can well stand in awe. It has evidently an objective existence carried on by a priestly caste. The majestic ritual of the Mass unfolds—needing no help from the individual worshipper. This corporate tradition makes no apologies for itself. It is secure in the possession of the sanction of the ages. Vestments are archaic, linking present to remote past. The language is that of ancient Rome, the language of Virgil and of Caesar, the language of mediaeval Christendom. The atmosphere and action connote memorial—a memory, in rite and ceremony, of the sacrifice central in Christian Faith. It brings to memory also saints and martyrs, and the countless worshippers who have said their

orisons at altar rail or shrine. Here worship is a strange
mingling of corporate oneness, and of individual prayer.
The bond between individual worshippers is not a shared
action, frequently not even a hymn, but membership in an
all-embracing institutional ritual. Half of the Christians in
the world are engaged in an exactly similar worshipping act.
At thousands of altars over the world the same words are
being said, the same vestments are being worn, the same
sonorous prayers are being directed to God. The Mass in
Catholic Christendom is a giant roll call—every member of
a world-wide community, on pain of mortal sin, presenting
himself at the House of Prayer. A Catholic Mass is one of
the most impressive sights in the world today. The religious
history of man probably has no more awesome exhibit of
corporate witness to a faith and to a cult. It is a fellowship
across all geographic boundaries. What is more, it is a fellowship across immeasurable time. It is the Church of historical tradition. It is the Church *in time*.

Yet the observer, if he brings with him a knowledge of
the Church of the New Testament, will miss many things.
There is here little reading of the Bible. Ritual action has
replaced words. There is no preaching, or very little, and
that not thought essential. There is no confession of Faith.
The worshipper's presence at the Church's cult-act takes
its place. Above all there is no parish fellowship—or again
very little. Communion is not thought of in communal terms.
Individuals go to the altar for the sacred host if properly
shriven in the Confessional, but of the Mass as a Holy Supper
of a people-Church there is no hint. The Church as the Body
of Christ, a mystery of fellowship, a life of *agape*, is strangely
absent. Catholic churchmanship means membership in a
world-wide organization, but the membership is atomistic,
each Christian largely for himself. Horizontal fellowship is

scarcely to be found. It is unity in a cult, not in a localized social reality.

In fact, as any observer may note, a middle term has dropped out in Catholic Church life. There is the great institutional Church. There is the individual. But the congregation is missing—the parish, the *Gemeinde*. Catholicism has, in a sense, the Great Church, a Church in history. It has lost, to a large extent, the Little Church, the local Family of God.

In an evangelical Church, on the other hand, this middle term is abundantly manifest. Here is the parish, the congregation. It is "Church" in the here and now—the New Testament *ecclesia* of Corinth or Thessalonica reborn. A Christian of the first century would recognize it. Here is the Bible and here is preaching. The ministry of the Word, indeed, has become central, as the place of the pulpit may indicate. Corporate fellowship, too, is everywhere evident. Hymns are corporately sung, and are one of the glories of Protestant Church life. Holy Communion has replaced the Catholic Mass. The very word Communion is stressed, since the Mass has become a corporate supper once more; individualistic communing would be an affront to the Body of Christ. If the Communion has become a rite of rare observance, this is partly owing to stress upon its corporate nature. It must be a parish communion or there must be none at all. Friedrich Heiler, a convert to Lutheranism from Rome, writes movingly of his first experience, in a Protestant Church, of congregational worship. His Catholic experience had left this manifestation of "Church" wholly a blank.[3] If a true doctrine of the Christian Church should mean merely the local, contemporary fellowship, the Protestant sect would have almost a monopoly of "Church" as over against Rome. W. G.

[3] Friedrich Heiler, *Evangelische Katholizität*, Munich, 1926, page 212.

Peck, commenting on the Methodist parish class-meetings can say: "Thus it came about that in Methodism, perhaps more than in any dissenting denomination, or even than in the Church of England, the individuals had the consciousness of belonging to the 'Body.' " [4]

But to return to our hypothetical observer. Granted that an evangelical Church service will impress him as embodying the Church as congregation, he will miss much also. The "Little Church" is here. But what about the "Great Church"? The evangelical worshipper is given little sense that he belongs to a corporate Body transcending his little group either in space or in time. The impression of contemporaneousness is foremost. The Church of history, with its wisdom of tradition, its symbols of corporate life in a Communion of Saints in time is largely lacking. The little flock here and now is alone. Few checks are in evidence upon whatever vagaries it may be tempted to practice. Contemporaneousness easily yields to secularity. At its worst, a Protestant service can differ little from a lecture in a city auditorium. Liturgical worship, in the sense of common sharing in an action, is replaced by a kind of word sacerdotalism. The "Little Church" is often cheated of its communal privileges (except for the singing of hymns). Evangelical worship denies its own principles. Vinet, speaking of Reformed worship, says: "It is remarkable that in our worship passivity predominates, while activity distinguishes the Catholic!" [5] Samuel Johnson's oft-quoted comment on Protestant worship is biting: "Sir, the Presbyterians have no public worship: they have no form of prayer in which they know they are

---

[4] W. G. Peck, *The Coming Free Catholicism*, Macmillan, 1919, page 124.

[5] Alexander Vinet, *Pastoral Theology*, Harper, 1853, page 179.

to join. They go to hear a man pray, and are to judge whether they will join with him."

As an Anglican I must hold my enthusiasm for the Book of Common Prayer severely in check. Is there anything essential in the Protestant *doctrine* of the Church which compels such neglect of the treasures of the Church of history? Is there not, in such exclusive attention upon contemporaneity a sinning against the fourth commandment: "Honor thy father and thy mother"? Is the cure for a divinized Church-in-history no contact with the Church of the ages at all? P. T. Forsyth confesses on behalf of Congregationalism: "We have starved ourselves of the rich treasury of Christian devotion in the profound and lovely liturgies of the long past, and of the wealth of example, inspiration, and guidance in the calendar of Christian sainthood." [6]

Is there anything essentially sinful in the Christian Year, in crosses, in the beauty of holiness, in using a prayer written by St. Chrysostom and repeated communally through many generations rather than a prayer written in the minister's study yesterday? Let the Protestant, by all means, preserve the element of freedom in Church life. But freedom unchecked by the Holy Spirit in the whole Body both in time and in the "now," can result in a loss of Christian Faith itself. The Bible can be lost—as it very nearly was in decadent Liberalism. The Great Church needs the Little Church. The Little Church needs the Great Church. The Church of God in its wholeness cries out for a rebirth and a revival.

I fear that my own convictions rather than those of a

[6] P. T. Forsyth, *The Church and the Sacraments*, Longmans, 1917, page 37. Vinet's similar comment could also be pertinent. Speaking of Rome, he says: "But its Liturgy, at least, does not dogmatize; it has the spirit of song, and therein it is good." See *Pastoral Theology*, page 180.

neutral observer have been voiced in the last paragraphs. But the subject tempts to emotional reactions. For the tragic schism between Great Church and Little Church seems unnecessary. A reformed, evangelical Great Church might have emerged in the sixteenth century. Doctrinally I would maintain that Reformation theology does not oppose it. Its failure to emerge was the result of inexperience, of blindness, of blunders. The Reformed Churches still have the Bible —a Bible gloriously rediscovered in our generation. The whole Church of God is in the Bible. Protestantism merely needs to return to its own first love and the ecumenical Church can come once more, a Church which some day might even conquer in love the proud citadel of Rome.

One thing more must be said before we dismiss our observer. A superficial judgment as between the two types of Church institutionalism might easily accord the promise of victory in the future to Catholicism. The latter possesses an external strength that can, if it is not opposed, leave the atomized fragments of non-Roman Christendom lying prostrate on the field of history. This prospect must mean for the Protestant Churches some form of unity or defeat. But such a tragedy can be averted. A united Kingdom of Christ can be reborn *in history*. First, to be sure, it must come in prophecy, in heart's desire, in doctrinal acceptance. Such acceptance involves no denial of the Reformation Gospel. The Reformation recovered the Church's anchorage in the Gospel. Christ was made, once more, Head of the Church. This momentous achievement need not be surrendered. In Rome, on the other hand (whatever one may say of other Catholicisms), a revival of a Gospel Church is confronted with what appear to be insuperable difficulties. For Rome has denied the priority of the Gospel and has enthroned an historical institutionalism in its stead. The Church of the Holy

Spirit has been displaced. There has been in Rome a *theological* apostasy.

This thesis will, I trust, become clearer as we proceed. Before dealing with the Catholic-Protestant chasm on its doctrinal side, however, I venture to present the testimony of a witness.

No theologian dealing with the doctrine of the Church in Anglicanism is today more influential than Frederick Denison ← Maurice. His *The Kingdom of Christ* (published still in two volumes in the Everyman Edition) has become a classic. Written a hundred years ago, it was far ahead of its time and is filled with prophecy. Maurice stood aloof from the Tractarian Catholic Movement in Anglicanism. Yet an evangelical Catholicism, such as he believed Anglicanism could, under God, exhibit, has perhaps never had a more valiant champion. He is probably the greatest theologian on the doctrine of the Church which Anglicanism has produced. This is what he says of the basic error of Roman Catholicism—that it divinizes itself and renounces submission to Christ, the Church's Lord: "It may sound like the strangest of all charges against Romanists to say that they have undervalued the Church; that they have thought meanly of it in relation to God and to man, of its work and of its powers. But I do believe that this is the very charge which we have most right to bring against both Latins and Greeks; it is for this sin, I hold, that they have been called, and will be called, to give account before the tribunal of Him who has committed to them their stewardship, and before those for whose use they have received it. Do you say, 'They have done their very utmost to exalt the Church; they have boasted of it as divine; they have said there was nothing in earth or heaven that it could not bind and loose; they have, till men became too enlightened to believe them, reduced their doctrine to practice, and made the priest the ruler over the spirits, souls, bodies of men'? Even so; your words are true; they establish my position. . . . When the Church's faith in its divine birth, in its regenerate position, in God's calling, was growing weak, then it must begin to say how very divine it is. When it no longer understands itself to be Christ, to be by its very nature and constitution spiritual, it must begin to assert that a certain mysterious spirituality had been conferred upon it apart from Christ; it must suppose that He had delegated His functions to those who should have seen that He was continually and in person exercising them; at last the notion must be adopted, and be regarded as necessary to the unity of the Church, that one person was representing Him in His absence, was His commissioned vicar." [7]

The Problem of Authority

The Catholic-Protestant chasm in Christendom is probably nowhere more obviously defined than in the divergent solution of the problem of authority. The papacy rules in Rome—a solution of the problem which obviates all further debate. But in Protestantism? Here no easy answer serves. Rome's boast is that Protestantism, by its very nature, cannot solve this problem and that, therefore, it is doomed.

Every corporate society wrestles with the problem of authority. It loomed large in the Old Testament. Who or what should rule the chosen people of God? God Himself? But through whom—king, or prophet, or priest? Or should God rule through a written law with a rabbi as interpreter? The Jewish people have tried, in turn, all of these solutions and are still a cohesive people—a nation in time if not in space.

[7] F. D. Maurice, *Theological Essays*, Macmillan, 1881, pages 205-206.

Had the New Testament Church been asked how it solved the problem of authority, it might have pointed to the Pentecostal event and the Church's consequent unity in the Holy Spirit. Christ through the Spirit ruled the Church. The greatest fruit of the Spirit was *agape*, Christian love. A society of *agape* is its own authority. *Agape*—the love of which St. Paul speaks—was then and is always a divine miracle, a theophany. It works miracles today. Hundreds of Christians, divided by walls of tradition and misunderstanding which seem, humanly speaking, unscalable, have in our ecumenical generation experienced its divine unifying power. In New Testament times it could humble even apostles. The Fellowship of *agape* could call both a Peter and a Paul to render accounts. Church order could grow up within the Fellowship; legalism could approach that of Judaism, cult-forms and liturgies could become inviolable tradition, and yet revolt was avoided. Even the schism between East and West was still a schism within Catholicism. It is an amazing fact, surely, that the deposit of unity with which the New Testament Church endowed the Church of history could endure until the sixteenth century, and carry burdens of corruption and secularization which historians hesitate to chronicle. For when the revolt came, the problem of authority had already found a dangerous solution. The Church of the Spirit had capitulated before the Church as institution. The Fellowship of *agape* had been mastered by an authoritarian hierarchy which refused to submit to judgment. The Fellowship had been silenced. What might not have resulted if, even within the framework of mediaeval Church life, a genuine ecumenical Church Council could have been held in the year 1520!

The subject of Church order must be left for separate treatment. But a general truth can, clearly, be drawn from

Roman Catholic Church history. The Church of history requires a norm to which it submits itself for judgment—and this norm cannot be the Church of history itself. Above all, it cannot be the institutional Church. There is nothing wrong (as I have argued earlier) with institutionalism as such. Even the most recent Pentecostal sect institutionalizes itself. But institutions are subject to all the demonic forces inherent in secular power. Power corrupts. Power requires humbling—always. Hence, when the authoritarian Church produced a hierarchy which assumed the title "Vicar of Christ," and actually functioned in such a vicarial capacity, the institution had become an idol.

The Protestant substituted Bible for pope. Did this solve the problem of authority? No, it did not. Catholicism has had an easy task in pointing to the failures of Biblicism. The Book as an idol can be as wrong as the pope. So can the substitution of intellectual dogma for a living covenant with God. Protestant orthodoxy has many sins to expiate. Nevertheless, the Reformers' appeal to Holy Scripture was essentially right. There is a once-for-all in Revelation—the mighty acts of God which founded the Church. Even the Holy Spirit, Third Person of the Trinity and dwelling in the Church, is derivative. He proceeds *from* the Father and the Son. The Church is not the Word of God. It is a creation of the Word of God.

The ultimate problem of religion is the problem of the Divine-Human encounter. It is the problem of bridging the gulf between holy divine love and human guilt. The Gospel is the drama of that bridging. Christ is the final Mediator. The Church is built on that Faith. The central doctrine of the Reformation, Justification by Faith, seized upon this insight. This doctrine has been misinterpreted often, but the whole Bible supports it. The essential meaning of it is that the gulf between man and God *has* been crossed. Christ's work has been accomplished. No further sacrifice is needed except the sacrifice of praise and thanksgiving. No good works are needed except as they are a necessary response to the acceptance, in penitence and faith, of the unearned love of God.

Now the error of Catholicism against which the Reformation protested, was that this Gospel was virtually denied. The gulf, so it said, has not been bridged once for all in Christ. The Church is a continuing Mediator. The Christ dwelling in the Church is still the suffering Christ, not the glorified Christ, sender of the Spirit. The Church must continue propitiation. Good works are required "in order to" bridge the gulf between God and guilt, not merely "because of" God's having already taken away the sins of the world.

Is there an evangelical solution to the problem of authority? I see none except the Fellowship of the Spirit itself, living under the judgment of Christ. To deny the Lordship of Christ is the real apostasy. This is the sin for which Maurice holds Rome to account. And Christ is known first of all in the Revelation recorded in the Bible. The Fellowship and the Bible belong together. The Bible as Book appeared within the Fellowship. It is, therefore, true to say that the Fellowship came first. The Fellowship was responsible for the Book. But the Fellowship is also responsible *to* the Book, for the Book contains the living Word of God to man. The Church, too, must submit to the Word. It was itself created by the Word. It must remain, in one sense, always creaturely. Yet when it submits to the Word, God can solve the problem of authority. To disdain institutionalism is not God's solution. It may take, precisely, realistic wrestling with institutions—with Church orders, with budgets, with sacramental practices—to recreate ecumenical Fellowship. When the ecumenical Fellowship under the

Word shall have been reborn, the Holy Spirit will be once more authority.

The Problem of Tradition

The problem of tradition is related to the problem of authority, and could be subsumed under it. Tradition is one of the forms under which the historical has become authority in the Church.

At first apostolic tradition was, indeed, authoritative. No New Testament had as yet been written. A great deal of the later succession doctrines in the Church arose from the simple necessity of preserving the Gospel message. Nor can the Church ever live in history without tradition. As was said earlier, Protestantism, insofar as it has tried to belittle tradition has starved itself of the life of the Holy Spirit Himself as He has unfolded His grace in the ongoing Fellowship.

The real problem of tradition arises when it is made equal to Revelation. The historical is always involved in sin. It is enmeshed in the temporal, the contingent. The Church is the holy people of God, but not everything which the Church does in meeting historical needs is holy. Nor ought such contingent truth become norm and be absolutized. Yet how easily this happens. Take mediaeval Christianity, with its popes and sacramental system, with its architecture and its mystical devotional life. All can be explained and even defended as historical developments taking shape under Providential guidance. Would any historian say that the early papacy may not have served the purposes of God?

But absolutize these historical developments and mischief results. When the Council of Trent pronounced anathema on anyone who refused to "receive and revere with an equal affection of piety and reverence" not only the written Scriptures but the traditions of the Church, it denied the further exercise of the very power by which tradition itself lives— God's ongoing rule in history. Tradition becomes frozen, or even dead. Indeed, so intolerable is such a condition that Rome, in later generations, had to create a safety valve. This is papal infallibility. History just will not stand still. If tradition is equated with Revelation, it has to have a master. Some organ of development has to be found. It is not always realized, I think, that the infallible papacy is precisely such an organ. Rome without papacy could not function. Pope Pius IX is reported to have said: *"La tradition c'est moi!"* (I am tradition). An English cardinal, after the Vatican Council of 1870, exclaimed: "Thank God, we are now done with tradition!" [8] Well, Rome is not quite "done with tradition." But Rome can manipulate tradition. Anyone noting papal disciplinary regulations on Lenten observance of fasting, for example, can discover that radical relaxation of traditional rules is being authorized. The rules remaining in force seem almost trivial. Rome is virtually admitting that mediaeval rigor was a mistake. The papacy can thus alter tradition. The Liturgical Movement, under the ægis of papal permissions, is introducing Reformation practices in liturgical life which seem revolutionary even to Anglo-Catholics.

It is, indeed, its failure to solve the problem of tradition which may turn out to be the flaw in Anglo-Catholicism. It desires to return to Catholic tradition. The Reformation settlement allows wide latitudes of interpretation. Ambiguities in that settlement can be utilized to permit a Church life which even approaches that of Rome. Yet the Reformation settlement accepted the Bible as authority and gave tradition a quite secondary place. Anglo-Catholicism has always

[8] Walter Lowrie, *The Church and Its Organization*, Longmans, 1904, page 65.

enjoyed honored privileges within the comprehensiveness of the Anglican communion. Tension became dangerous only with the Oxford Movement which began to champion pre-Reformation tradition as authority in its own right over against the later developments in Anglicanism. "Catholic" began to mean loyalty to a tradition in which the Anglican centuries since the Reformation, as well as the continental Reformation tradition, had been belittled or left out. "Church" began to be narrowed to include only that portion of Christendom which had remained loyal to the pre-Reformation Church order and sacramental system.

Anglo-Catholicism has had great appeal. As a leaven in Anglicanism it has been a blessing and a tutor unto godliness. But the moment it absolutizes tradition (an arbitrarily selected portion of tradition, be it remembered) it encounters resistance or even hostility. Anglican conscience begins to call a halt. Here, it feels, is the error of Rome all over again, even though the content of tradition may be only a mild version of the Roman system. A host of illustrations could serve—the system of seven sacraments, the sacerdotal eucharist, the word "Mass," the designation "Father" for minister, the revival, in disciplinary and compulsory form, of the sacrament of penance. Traditional Anglicanism has not really rebelled against these and many other revivals in cult or practice so long as they were not doctrinally defined as authoritative. For the moment they are defined as authoritative, the prior problem of the dogmatic value of tradition itself is raised. And on this issue the Reformation settlement is *un*ambiguous. It is on the Protestant side. Anglo-Catholicism then ceases to be an illustration of the comprehensiveness of Anglicanism, but becomes Counter-Reformation—a very different thing. Authority, for Anglo-Catholicism, then, is no longer the living Fellowship within which it leads a permitted and even encouraged life, but a Fellowship outside or prior to Reformation Anglicanism. Were dogmatic Anglo-Catholicism to win control of the Anglican Churches, honesty might compel it, sooner or later, to repeal Anglican Reformation formularies.

But even a victory would not really solve the problem of authority. Anglo-Catholicism has no pope. Tradition could become a tyrant. Just where in history would you absolutize it? At the close of the period of ecumenical Church Councils, as does Eastern Orthodoxy? But Anglo-Catholicism has accepted Roman tradition far beyond this point. At the pre-Reformation period? At the Council of Trent, without the pope? At the stage of Roman development short of 1870? It could not appeal to contemporary ecumenical authority, since, unless readmitted by Rome, or turned Eastern Orthodox, its doctrine of tradition would not permit subjecting itself to a corporate judgment which had not itself first submitted to tradition.

The main stream of Anglicanism has welcomed Anglo-Catholicism hitherto, and this for many good reasons. An *ecumenical* Anglo-Catholicism would, I believe, be welcomed by the whole of non-Roman Christendom. What could it not do to reintroduce into modern Christianity the richness of the Church of history. Most evangelical Anglicans could at the same time be called Liberal Anglo-Catholics. But the more dogmatic Anglo-Catholicism may exclude itself from the ecumenical Church if it does not surrender its doctrine of authority. It may some day face a decisive choice. Either it will submit itself to the corporate judgment of the emerging ecumenical Fellowship (let alone of the larger Anglican Fellowship within which it still lives) or it may run the danger of becoming a sect.

One illustration, perhaps, will serve. The prevailing custom among most Anglicans had long dropped the mediaeval rule of fasting before Holy Communion. It is not prescribed in the Prayer Book. Indeed, traditional Anglicanism had come to share the custom general in Reformation Churches of not too frequent Communions, since these were held to require careful preparation. Communions, when held, were at the traditional Sunday late-morning hour. No doubt, infrequency of Communions had gone much too far—as many Protestant leaders admit on all sides today. Yet great values inhered in this custom—particularly in its insistence that the Holy Supper was a corporate rite. For the sake of preserving its corporate nature and its status as an awesome assembling of the Body of Christ at the holy table, the fault of infrequency was endured. I would make no defense of infrequency. The Reformers themselves pleaded for frequency, as one of the classic exhortations in the Anglican Book of Common Prayer can prove. But corporateness was the first requirement. And a glorious recovery of the doctrine of the Church lies behind this Reformation emphasis. A sacerdotal Mass, without the Fellowship partaking, was judged unchurchly. During the Middle Ages, however, Communion had become increasingly rare, to the point where the average parishioner did not commune more frequently than once in several years. Winning the people-Church back to the holy table proved to be too difficult a revolution of custom. Hence the insistence on corporateness paid the price of infrequency.

The Anglo-Catholic Counter-Reformation went back for guidance to pre-Reformation tradition. Here was the Mass in its sacerdotal grandeur. Here was the altar fenced about by disciplines, particularly those of fasting preparation and the Confessional. How to revive these and yet fit them into Reformation Anglicanism has been a complex problem. A

variety of solutions has been the result. Evangelical Anglicanism, having neglected a true insight into a doctrine of the
Church and having yielded largely to pietistic individualism,
has not had a program based on principle with which
competently to counter-balance or criticize the Counter-
Reformation Movement. A whole series of dangerous misunderstandings are consequently appearing in the Anglican
Church family. One finds, in some Anglican parishes, a self-
conscious differentiation between those who observe fasting
preparation and those who do not; between those who attend
an early morning eucharist and neglect the parish service,
and those who cling to the traditional "Morning Prayer."
From the point of view of a corporate concept of the Church,
the most dangerous development is perhaps the neglect of a
corporate Holy Supper altogether, since insistence on fasting discipline may prevent communicating at the late-
morning eucharist, a non-communicating "Mass" taking its
place. Parishioners have a choice between receiving Communion at an early service, to which they come fasting, or
not receiving at all. This early morning service is usually one
without hymns and without sermon. Its appeal for the devout
is great. It wins to individualistic prayer and parallels the
mystic winsomeness of Roman Catholic worship. Yet here
lies its danger. The Church as Body, as a people of God, may
disappear from view. Eastern Orthodoxy, true to a more
primitive tradition, has never permitted "low" eucharists.
A great insight into the primitive doctrine of the Church
lies behind that refusal. In Anglicanism differences regarding
preparation for Communion can lead to a breaking of the
basic Communion—the Church—itself!

The debate on a detail in discipline illustrates the dangers
lurking in treating any tradition as an absolute. Preparation
for a Holy Supper could well be accepted as a necessary

discipline in Church life. Fasting can surely be such a discipline. The danger comes in absolutizing the form. Traditions grow up in history; they are conditioned to the life of an epoch, or to an historical need. Tradition needs a master, or else one period of Church history tyrannizes over another. Why, for example, should not post-Reformation tradition have its rights also? The Church is a living Body. A living tradition, with roots in the past, is a rock of strength to any corporate society. Anglo-Catholicism did a great service to Anglicanism in bringing forth "treasures old." But the moment it refuses to share these with "treasures new," or turns tradition into a tyrannical master, it endangers the prior unity of the Body of Christ itself. Protestantism is guilty of ignoring many of the values of tradition. It is guilty also when it permits Biblical literalism to tyrannize over the Church of history. But it is right in the humility which its return to Holy Scripture as norm can mean. The twentieth of the Anglican Articles of Religion contains much Reformation wisdom: "It is not lawful for the Church to ordain any thing that is contrary to God's word written, neither may it so expound one place of Scripture, that it be repugnant to another. Wherefore, although the Church be a witness and a keeper of Holy Writ, yet, as it ought not to decree anything against the same, so *besides the same ought it not to enforce anything to be believed for salvation.*" The Bible binds, but it also sets free.

The problem of fasting before Communion, used as an illustration of an absolutized tradition, is, to be sure, complicated by doctrinal considerations—particularly by the Catholic-Protestant disagreement regarding the doctrine of sacramental grace. Its chief bearing upon a doctrine of the Church, however, consists in illuminating the tension between the living contemporary people of God and an in-

stitutionalism absolutized in history. Rome, as indicated
earlier, solves this tension through the papacy. The fasting
discipline is being modified by papal dispensations in as-
toundingly liberalized ways today. Evening communions
are multiplying in the Roman Church, and the Liturgical
Movement makes radical proposals regarding the fasting discipline generally. The point is that legalized tradition simply
dare not be permitted to become master of the Church.
Tradition, too, can become an idol.

Bible Fundamentalism and dogma Fundamentalism can
be as dangerous as tradition Fundamentalism. Bible Fundamentalism has been, for twentieth-century theology, pretty
well dissolved. Tradition Fundamentalism still may need
humbling. That is why the Reformation Churches, with their
return to the Bible, are potentially safer today than perhaps
they ever were. God may have permitted both Reformation
and the critical enlightenment of later centuries to happen in
order to prepare for a truly ecumenical Church. On either
side idolatries had to be smashed. The ecumenical Church
today can approach the problem of tradition with a solution
in its hands as could the Church in no previous period of history. It can have the reopened Bible and it can, if it will,
have the treasures of tradition, both Catholic and Protestant.
It can be the Kingdom *in history*. Its fragments can reunite,
having "One Lord, one faith, one baptism, one God and
Father of all. . . ." For "unto every one of us is given grace
according to the measure of the gift of Christ."

The Word of God as authority *to* the Church; the Holy
Spirit working through brotherly love as authority *in* the
Church—are not these the two foci of authority to be found
in the New Testament *ecclesia*? St. Paul's epistles evidence
one long struggle to protect these authorities against attack.
No battle in later Church history has been more important

than the battle against the tyranny of Jewish legalistic tradition fought out in the apostolic era. To maintain unity with freedom under the Gospel is, admittedly, difficult. Yet the ecumenical movements of our own time prove that visions of a free yet catholic Church need not be illusory. Christian love under the Gospel—has it ever been fully tried? C. S. Lewis, in his *Screwtape Letters,* has the master of devils comment on Anglican churchmanship strife: "You would expect to find the 'low' churchman genuflecting and crossing himself lest the weak conscience of his 'high' brother should be moved to irreverence, and the 'high' one refraining from these exercises lest he should betray his 'low' brother into idolatry. And so it would have been but for our ceaseless labour. Without that, the variety of usage within the Church of England might have become a positive hotbed of charity and humility." [9] Christian brotherliness as itself the foremost Christian tradition! That this solution of the problem of authority scarcely ever dawns upon our conscience may be a sobering commentary on our loss of a true Biblical doctrine of the Church of God.

The Liturgy

The Catholic-Protestant chasm has been explored thus far in this chapter only very partially. The chasm, in fact, is better described as a canyon traversing a plain—wide here, narrow there. The silt of the centuries has levelled the gulf in places. Elsewhere it is wider than ever, and may long remain unbridgeable. Rome demands submission. The Reformed Churches demand repentance and reformation. The Liturgical Movement within Rome is a sign that reform is not impossible within the Mother Church of western Chris-

[9] C. S. Lewis, *The Screwtape Letters,* Macmillan, 1943, pages 84–85.

tendom. A New Testament doctrine of the Church, a re-discovery of the meaning of the Church as the Body of Christ, runs through that movement. This could bring heal-ing to the separated peoples of God. Yet the Liturgical Movement is in its infancy and may soon wither as it, too, encounters the dogma of tradition under the mastery of an infallible pope.

This same Liturgical Movement, however, gives promise of one area in which Catholic and Protestant could meet and share the same riches of God's grace. This is the wor-ship life of the Christian people of God.

It would take far more learning than I possess to explain some of the riddles which the history of liturgical worship and practice must present to the historian of the Christian Church. Why was this treasure so generally lost during the Protestant exodus? Why was the Anglican Church the only Reformation Church to write and to live by a Book of Common Prayer? It had required all the centuries of Christian history since the apostles to garner that treasure. Liturgical prayer is not produced in a day or by one genera-tion. Theological genius does not suffice. No individual, however gifted, can do more than contribute a small portion. Liturgy is a community possession. It grows only in the soil of a long tradition, nurtured in that soil by thousands and millions of Christian hearts lifted up in common orison. Only a Spirit-bearing Body can create liturgical worship—and only if it lives a life in time. A living tradition has been defined as "the pulse of the timeless in time." [10]

"Almighty God, unto whom all hearts are open, all de-sires known, and from whom no secrets are hid: Cleanse the thoughts of our hearts by the inspiration of thy Holy Spirit,

[10] James Moffatt, *The Thrill of Tradition*, Macmillan, 1944, page 3. This book is wise.

that we may perfectly love thee, and worthily magnify thy holy Name."

Thus opens the Catholic Mass (in the Sarum rite, upon which the Book of Common Prayer is largely based). Where did these moving words come from? Nobody knows. Their origin is shrouded in the mists of tradition. They long ante-date the "errors of Rome." No Reformation needed to re-volt against them. Like scores of similar prayers, like the dialogue of the Eucharist itself, they have sung themselves into the memories of generation upon generation of wor-shippers. A mere visitor to a liturgical Church can with difficulty comprehend what they can mean to those whose inmost possession they have become. Such a visitor may be shocked at the manner in which the minister "patters" the liturgy—and this is a grave fault, one may grant, on the minister's part. Yet the visitor might be surprised how little this matters to the liturgically minded parishioners. This is *their* prayer, not the minister's. It is *Common* Prayer. Lips move, or if not lips, then hearts, in a common chorus. There may be a place in the worship service where the minister can voice *his* individual petition for his flock. Free Church worship has "treasures new," which liturgical worship needs to incorporate or add. But the genius of liturgical worship would be shattered by individualistic intrusions. The Church as Spirit-moved Body prays.

And so with liturgical action. It has become formalized, no doubt, and this exposes it to great dangers. It is a curious paradox that in Romanist worship even the prayers are not vocally shared and are frequently not even heard, since they are in an ancient language. Formalism has smothered paro-chial participation. But this is not true liturgical worship. Formalism is a vice, an ever-present snare in all communal ritual. Mrs. Elizabeth Fry, a Quaker, once wrote in her

journal: "Bitter experience has proved to me that Friends do
rest too much on externals." [11] Formlessness, when grown
traditional, is also form. That is why the ministry of the
Word is so essential in all Christian assemblies. It can pierce
the armor of convention. It can speak the Word of God over
against the Church. It can rouse conscience and destroy
complacency. It can guard against the ever-present danger
in Catholic types of worship—that of mysticism. Mysticism
(I use the word somewhat technically) is always in danger
of escaping the life of the community, as also of ignoring
the gulf between God and guilt which prevents man's ab-
sorption into holy deity.[12] But the true nature of liturgical
action—a baptism or a eucharist—is, precisely, that of a communal drama, realistic, historical. True liturgical worship
is not mystical.

Many reasons could be ventured as to why Protestantism,
by and large, lost liturgical worship. The Reformers were
theologians and not liturgical experts. They knew little of
the historic roots of the liturgical life of the Church. It is, in
fact, only within recent generations that liturgical scholarship has unearthed the pertinent documents. No one in the
early days of the Church thought it worth while to record
living and growing tradition. Furthermore, the real genius
of liturgy had been lost in the mediaeval period. The infrequency of participation on the part of the people in the Communion has already been mentioned. The Mass had become
a sacerdotal monopoly. The people had to be content with
sight of the action. The monstrance with its consecrated
host became the focus of adoration, not the corporate rite of
the holy table. The Liturgical Movement in Roman Cathol-

[11] James Moffatt, *The Thrill of Tradition*, page 140.
[12] See Emil Brunner's important book, *Die Mystik und das Wort*,
Tübingen, 1928, particularly the closing chapter.

icism is belatedly trying to correct these long-entrenched errors. At any rate, most of the Reformation Churches, while they revived the people-Church, did not recover a true understanding of liturgy. The Word service had been redis-covered. Its power was so novel and moving that loss of the action service was not felt. Sacraments had lost in the me-diaeval period much of their anchorage in corporate life and feeling. The Church as Fellowship largely existed with-out them. Hence, here too, the Reformation merely carried over a neglect.

The Liturgical tradition of the period immediately before the Reformation was a debased tradition. The Reformers rightly saw errors in it, without realizing that concealed under many errors was a treasure derived from the early Church. The Catholic Mass itself is much older than the scholastic theology which overlaid it with interpretations. Evangelical theology may have to reform it, yet when it is seen against the background of the fifth century, instead of the fifteenth, the Catholic liturgy is the worship deposit of the classic centuries of Christendom—the very age to which the Reformers themselves wished to return. Historical my-opia prevented their seeing this. Cranmer and his English colleagues, by an accident of history, were equipped with liturgical scholarship sufficient to avoid spilling the baby with the bath. They could rescue and reform.

All this and more can be offered as an excuse for the loss of liturgical tradition in most Reformation churches. One may add that absolutizing the worth of liturgy is itself wrong. Liturgy is not all of Church existence. It can become an end in itself and be the Church at self-worship. Protestantism, with its passion for ethical expression of the Gospel and for the ministry of the Word, is a greatly needed corrective upon all mere devoutness—though the correction applies more to a false mystical liturgical development than to true corporate worship action.

Nevertheless, a loss there was. And it is in overcoming or bridging this loss that Anglicanism may have made one of its most valuable contributions to the ecumenical Christianity of the future. We of the Anglican Churches do have the greatest Reformation liturgical achievement—the Book of Common Prayer. We have lived by it for centuries and can testify to its enduring grace. It has been for us a bond of peace and a stir to righteousness of life. What little we know of a doctrine of the Church, as the New Testament embodies this, we owe largely to the Prayer Book. Here is one link with Catholicism, particularly early Catholicism, which is marvelous in our sight. It is the cause of our being proud of a Catholic as well as a Protestant heritage.

The Anglican Churches could say to the other Reformation Churches: "We owe you debts we can never repay. We joined you in the exodus from Egypt, and woe be unto us if we are lured by memory of fleshpots back to slavery under a false Church authority. We owe to you our own recovery of the Gospel, our Bible, many of our hymns, our ministry of the Word. We produced no giant theologians comparable to Luther or Calvin. Doctrinal insights have been with us largely derivative, softened versions of your more embattled faiths. But one gift was granted us (two, if Catholic Church order be included). We became a fully Reformed Church comparatively late. We were a pragmatic people and revolt from the Roman Mother Church took milder forms than yours. We retained bridges across the ecclesiological schism of the sixteenth century. The prayer tradition of the Catholic centuries is one of these bridges. This tradition we believe to be true, not false, tradition. The learned doctors and authoritarian popes of the Middle Ages had little to

do with it. It derives from a much older source—from the
days of the Church's martyrs and from the time when it
cost men something to belong to the people of God. It is the
living sacrament of a holy people, generation linked to generation, across the fissures of time and across geographical
alienations. The very name, Book of Common Prayer, we
believe to symbolize what the apostles meant by the Communion of saints and by the community of the Holy Spirit.

"This Book we owe to our Fathers as you of the other
Reformation Churches owe your insights to yours. We
caught from your Reformers a vision of a people-Church,
a vision of a congregation no longer under sacerdotal tyranny. Our Reformation elders also wanted such a Little
Church, the Christian parish, gathered to hear the awesome
word of God and to partake of the meal of the Kingdom
around a holy table. Whenever we have lost sight of the
Christian congregation as truly the home of the Spirit, we
must confess error. But we supplemented insight into the
meaning of the Little Church by a vision of the Great
Church in which the Little Church can find a larger home.
This is what we mean when we gladly preserve the name
Catholic as well as Protestant or Reformed. Our experience
testifies to the fact that there can be an assembly of the
Great Church as well as of the local congregation. Common
Prayer, shared in a thousand households of God, is a great
assembly. Its voice goes forth unto everlasting. Our Great
Church is not yet the ecumenical Church. It is but a foretaste of this. But we have found in this Church of history
a refuge and a strength. It humbles us daily. Its tradition of
the Christian Year, for example, constitutes a kind of Fifth
Gospel. It is the story of God's redemption liturgically made
present over and over again. It is the Bible become drama in
worship form. Without such anchorage in tradition, we see

many a Church losing itself in pursuit of modern substitutes which cheapen the Gospel or even lose it. The Creeds, too, find in the setting of liturgical worship their happy and rightful throne. Are they not confessions of the Church of our Fathers and of yours, shields once used against giant enemies of the Faith? We rejoice to recite them, but with no insistence that they are complete statements of Christian truth or are untouchable by reverent criticism."

Such, though it be but a fragment of a full report, might be an Anglican's testimonial accounting of the gifts he hopes to bring to the ecumenical Household of God. He, too, has not healed the Catholic-Protestant schism. Treasures of Christian Faith would be jeopardized in a premature healing. The Reformation Churches find an angel with a flaming sword guarding the gateway against a return to Rome or to any idolizing of an infallible tradition. Yet the ecumenical Church of the future needs tradition. Our world cries aloud for World Churchmanship. It would be a tragedy if such World Churchmanship were attempted without recovering first our roots in the past.

John Foster, the Methodist missionary whom I quoted in the opening pages of this book, illustrates the crying need of tradition in the younger Churches of our world-expanded Christianity.

"I have been appalled," he says, "at the results of transferring some worship traditions, away from the environment which produced them, to a young church in a non-Christian land. It has led to horrible irreverences when raw congregations have been led straight into 'free' worship. No ingrained habits of reverence, no steeping in the devotions of the Psalter, no deep knowledge of New Testament scriptures, no worthy hymn-book long contributing to the language of prayer, no experience of the discipline of a liturgy.

The result too often is a meeting, with a 'chairman,' a little opening prayer—very little, because folk soon begin to shuffle and the main talk is not yet—noisy hymns, prelude to a long address. . . . To regard that as passing on one's worship tradition is surely to do injustice to one's spiritual ancestors."

"At one time," so the author continues in a later paragraph, "I was responsible for daily worship in a Chinese college chapel. Morning and evening we used the sort of daily office in which mediaeval monks raised their souls to God. Some of my colleagues were surprised at this in a non-Anglican! But surely the conflicts of the past, and the consequent tenderness of some of our private feelings, must not be allowed to rob us of the Book of Common Prayer as the link by which we *all* are joined on to the Church of the West in its pre-Reformation period. . . . When one remembers that the prayers are full of Biblical phrases, the responses are verses of the Psalms, the canticles are all from the Bible except the *Te Deum* (which is itself strongly Biblical and undoubtedly inspired), and that the creed is merely a summary of Biblical facts, one realizes that this traditional form of public worship is more thoroughly scriptural than anything which has come to take its place. Why should not anyone—anyone—be free to return? At any rate, I felt that I was standing for 'the experience of the Universal Church,' and standing for it as that which fills up the negative aspects, corrects the partial emphases, of the narrower denominational position." [13]

Such words are flattering to Anglicans, and we rejoice in them. May Anglicans, however, receive the needed grace to yield their pride in non-essentials of faith and practice so

[13] John Foster, *Then and Now*, Student Christian Movement Press, 1942, pages 54-56.

that at least this treasure of historic Catholicism—Common Prayer—may find acceptance in the ecumenical Fellowship which God is calling into being in our time.

Conclusion

Dr. William L. Sullivan, noted Protestant preacher, a convert at the age of thirty-seven from the Roman Catholic Church, in which he had been a member of a religious order, describes in his autobiography what "Church" means to a Catholic: "The Church is his aristocracy and romantic love; his household, where he mingles with the holiest of all the ages, children, like himself, of a mother solicitous and majestic, nurse of saints, yet mindful of her sinners, and keeping in her heart memories incomparable, so far back as the age of martyrs and the missions of the Apostles. When she takes him to her embrace, he ceases to be a casual atom of humanity; he becomes an heir of the ages, a citizen in the commonwealth of God; his name thence-forward is entered in the vastest brotherhood ever known on earth, and written through this august mediation in the book of life above. The Church has saved civilization and will save him, for her mission is to save. For the mind she has light, for the soul sanctity, for death consolation and a ministration of an immortality of beatitude. Where is any likeness to her to be found?" [14]

Dr. Sullivan introduces his words with the assertion that such a concept of the Church is "next to impossible for a Protestant to understand." Most Protestants would have to admit that Dr. Sullivan's judgment is at least partly right. The very word "Church," in Protestant imagination, has been poisoned by the memory of ancient wars between the

[14] William L. Sullivan, *Under Orders*, Richard R. Smith, 1944, page 36.

sects. Yet is Dr. Sullivan's indictment of Protestantism wholly right? Change a word or two in his glowing tribute. Then apply it to the memory every Protestant has of the congregation of Christian souls in which he was ushered into the grace of Christ. It may have been humble and unadorned, but it had its hymns and its Bible and its fellowship of prayer and communal piety, its expressions of brotherhood and service. Could he not describe the meaning of Church much as does the Catholic? The difference lies in the more universal corporate life which the Catholic can experience— "the holiest of *all* the ages," "memories incomparable," "heir of the ages." The Protestant is more likely to be limited to an experience of an isolated flock or the relatively narrow confines of a sect or a denomination.

But need the Protestant be thus limited? Is not the history of the people of God a common heritage? Exodus from a Church which had assumed vested rights in that heritage could be in the name of the truer heritage itself. Luther and Calvin frequently speak of the Church of the Fathers. Protestants have been blind to their own rights in the inheritance bequeathed to them, as to Rome or any other fraction of the people of God, by the saints and martyrs and repentant sinners of the long procession of the Christian generations.

An analogy leaps to mind here. If the doctrine of states' rights had won out during our American Civil War, the nation would have suffered a schism. Further schisms, indeed, might have ensued. What would the concept "America" have meant to the seceding newer nations? Undoubtedly the fractional America retaining the ancient seat of government, with its sacramental symbols of sovereignty, such as the great seal and the historic flag, would have claimed a monopoly of American tradition. And the newer nations, eager to establish fresh loyalties, might have yielded to such pretensions. But a day would surely have come when a sense of American unity could arise once more. Then the shared heritage of the history preceding schism (or even during schism) could be rediscovered as a common treasure. The most powerful motive for reuniting could well be the fact that, though separated outwardly, the fragmented Americas were still one in basic faith and loyalties, in the sharing of a common vocation as a "new nation, conceived in liberty, and dedicated to the proposition that all men are created equal."

An analogy like the above has obvious dangers. The principles involved in the break-up of a united Christendom are not to be equated with the causes of the Civil War, though Roman Catholic polemic has often interpreted them as not much different. Such complexities may be ignored. The point is that the separated Churches of Christ simply cannot read one another out of the "Church" as the one people of God. The break in fellowship can be traced to failure in repentance on the part of a mother institution or to self-pride in an offspring sect. We have, however, led separated existences long enough to learn that the call to repentance comes to all of us now. No historical embodiment of "Church," though it may have broken away under an undeniable compulsion of conscience, can boast of escape from the same judgment it felt called upon to voice against its parent institution. By now "all have sinned and come short of the glory of God."

The first step toward a united people of God is the rediscovery of our common heritage in basic Apostolic faith. And to this must be added our common heritage in the history of the people of God to whom that faith was entrusted. We share a common vocation—and a common judgment. We have been and are a sinful people, as were the people of God of the old covenant. God may have found no better tool of judgment for a sinning Church than the smashing of its unity. The Reformation was such a tool in the hand of God for Rome, and led Rome to at least a partial reform. To cite another example, the exodus of Methodism from a blind Church of England was a similar act of judgment. Nor is the story of broken households of faith ended. But woe to a tool which presumes upon the God who uses it. "Shall the ax boast itself against him that heweth therewith? or shall the saw magnify itself against him that shaketh it?" "Wherefore it shall come to pass that when the Lord hath performed his whole work upon mount Zion and on Jerusalem, I will punish the stout heart of the king of Assyria, and the glory of his high looks" (Isaiah 10:15,12).

Protestantism has boasted that it brought judgment upon a proud unrepentant institution. But has it taken to heart the possibility that the role of judge and judged could be reversed? Protestantism, in its turn, may have presumed against God. No "remnant" gathered out of the people of the old covenant was thereby spared the judgments visited upon the nation. It was called to be a saving, not a saved remnant. Schisms within the Body of Christ will not be healed until we share one another's guilt as well as one another's gifts of grace. The corruptions of mediaeval Rome are those of our own forefathers in the family of God. The faith of those centuries produced the Reformation. In our own time, no sect or denomination can arrogate to itself the promises of Christ for His Church.

Shared repentance alone can begin to atone for the sins of schism. Repentance is still the common bond uniting all members of the Body of Christ. *Kyrie eleison!* Lord have mercy upon us! We meet in unity before the ultimate throne of forgiveness. But we meet there as individuals. Could we meet there as churches too? Has history ever seen a truly

repentant *church?* Must the phrase "moral man and im-
moral society" apply to the Church as to secular social
orderings? The disunity of Christendom is so glaring a sin
that a gathering of repentant churches may come to pass.
There is, indeed, no escape from this hard solution. If, under
God's rule over His people, this miracle could happen, even
the centuries of disunity would find redemption in a new,
undreamt of dawn for the Kingdom of Christ.

IV

THE PROBLEM OF CHURCH ORDER

Whenever an ecumenical discussion takes place, it is usually not long before the problem of the ministry becomes a topic of debate. At least this is true if an Anglican or a representative of some other Catholic Church order is present. The doctrine of the ministry—and the related doctrine of the sacraments—is the area of sharpest division in ecumenical controversy. On other issues agreements are frequently possible. Or, if disagreements remain, these do not necessarily break Christian understanding and fellowship. But the doctrine of the ministry is seldom treated as indifferent. Schemes for Church reunion must solve this problem or fail. No Christian Church would place its own doctrine of the ministry exactly at the head of its doctrinal system of belief. Neither bishops, nor priests, nor deacons, nor presbyteries and synods, are mentioned in the classic creeds— a fact which should be of some importance. Yet Christian unity demands more than oneness in basic faith. It demands sacramental corporate expression. The "Breaking of Bread" antedates, as a symbol of Church life, New Testament or formalized creeds. It is the fundamental act of Christian fellowship. Breaking of bread together implies some kind of Church order. Someone must actually *break* the bread for the Family of God. Church order is of the essence of Church life. Regardless of the fact that Christian Faith rests on foundations which may be doctrinally separated from the historic Christian Fellowship, and may be, in some sense, prior to the life of the Fellowship in history, as soon as the Church enters the story of Revelation, Church order is there. Belittlement of the problem of Church order belittles the Church of God.

Yet, as any Christian churchman studies the ecumenical debates of the past generation, how hopeless appears a solution to this problem! Hundreds of Christian communions, each with its own Church order! If Christian reunion hinges upon unifying the ecclesiastical orderings of Christendom, ecumenical theology may well be baffled. The problem is so complex that no exploration of it can do more than untangle a few knots. Yet, in humble submission to the vocation of our day of the Lord, all Christians are called to contribute to the task. Even naïve attempts may help. They can rouse imagination and conscience.

One of our great needs is that this whole matter of the ministry should be viewed in a large perspective. It cries out for the application of common sense and of imaginative analogy. The doctrine of the ministry has become surrounded with taboos. A Protestant, for example, finds it wellnigh impossible to view Apostolic Succession or the historic episcopate fairly because he sees these only through the value-judgments which have been given to them in Catholic polemic. Let him, so he fears, admit Apostolic Succession and he reads himself out of the ministry. The Catholic, in turn, finds it equally impossible to avoid reading back into the second century the Church order he lives under today. "Bishop" and "priest" mean something so definitely "Catholic" that he would be shocked to see his ancestral ministry as it probably was in actuality—a ministry resembling a Congregationalist or Presbyterian Church order far more than contemporary Catholicism. Both Protestant and Catholic could profit from a fresh historic approach.

One of the undervalued yet important clues to an understanding of the problem of Church order and of the grievous controversies surrounding it is the one already mentioned—the corporate act common to all but a fraction of Christendom, the Holy Supper. I shall venture to exploit this clue in much of the argument of this chapter. It goes far toward explaining the rise of the episcopate in the early Church, as of the subsidiary orders of presbyterate and diaconate. The Holy Communion is a common denominator even today in all Church orders, however diverse they may appear on the surface. An observer, freed from controversial prejudice, might surely be more than a little amazed at the uniformity which still underlies the apparent chaos of Church orderings since the Reformation.

Take Congregational Church order as an example—or better that of Independency generally, since this could include a number of denominations which have the congregational theory of Church polity in common. Every such independent congregation still has a minister. He is "breaker of bread" for the Christian "gathered" group, fulfilling, in addition, such other functions as naturally fall to the presiding father of a family united in table fellowship. For the sake of analogy with more complex Church orders, let us give to such a minister the generic title of "bishop." This is not absurd, since many a second-century Christian bishop may well have ruled over not more than a single congregation. Our congregational bishop fulfills in the "Little Church" many, if not most, of the functions which the Catholic bishop of traditional Church order exercises in the "Great Church." Independency is Catholicism reduced in scale. As a recent writer, a Congregationalist, declares: "The concept of the 'Independent' Church needs to be re-examined and re-stated. When this is done, we are sure that apparently irreconcilable points of view will be seen to be much nearer each other than we had ever realized. . . . To call a Church an 'Independent' Church is to say that it is a 'Catholic' Church—a church, that is, which bears all the marks of the Church's catholicity upon itself and does not need, therefore, to derive any spiritual sustenance or authority from outside its own life. . . . We have not realized that the Church Order of traditional Catholicism is, in fact, that of 'Independency.' . . . A Diocese is a large-scale model of an 'Independent' Church, just as a modern properly organized Congregational Church is a small-scale model." [1]

Now, I might not agree with the writer's assertion that an Independent Church "bears all the marks of the Church's catholicity upon itself." "Independent" and "Catholic" cannot thus be equated. Almost the whole ecumenical problem consists in the fact that they are still antithetic. But the analogy between "Little Church" and "Great Church" is valid and important. The "bishop" of the Little Church, for example, was not created merely by a single congregation, however much the independent flock may have determined his election and call. Even in Independency the minister is ordained by other ministers—normally by at least three other "bishops," who, in their turn, have similarly received denominational rather than merely local orderings and thus stand in an historic succession. This succession is not recognized by Catholic Churches; it is often not very much valued by Independency itself; it may even be belittled or almost denied in doctrine. But it is still there in practice and may mean more to Independency than official pronouncements reveal. The congregation, after it has received its

[1] Daniel T. Jenkins, *The Nature of Catholicity*, Faber and Faber, 1942, pages 104–106.

"bishop" may be independent enough. But it is still dependent upon other congregations to secure a minister in the first place. Exceptions exist, I admit. The most striking exception occurs, as a rule, when a new sect is historically launched. A Founder may appear and assume an apostolic role and function. He plants Churches by himself. The Founder usually is himself originally in a corporate succession, but he breaks away and begins a new one. Yet when a new denomination has been launched, the Founder's privilege is not handed on. The traditional "Catholic" form of ministerial ordering takes over. A little Catholicism has once more been born and takes its place as a rival to the hundreds already in existence.

Is it fanciful to see in each denominational Church ordering a reduplication, in miniature, of the episcopal system of the Church of Catholic history? I think not. The break-up of Catholic Christendom into sectarianism has not destroyed all similarity of structure. It has, however, broken it into smaller fragments. The diocese has become the congregation. The Great Church has become a congeries of Little Churches. Anglicanism differs from the denominational Churches in that it broke with the Great Church of pre-Reformation days, not by way of a single Founder, but by way of a corporate secession. It had three bishops to start its new succession. And these bishops were diocesan, not parish "bishops." What this distinction may mean must be left for later discussion.

Another analogy, as well as difference, between Great Church and Little Church deserves mention. Every Church in Christendom has both a Church order and a Church polity. The term "Church order" describes the basic structure of flock and shepherd. This is carried on or transplanted by a ministerial succession and a sacramental rite of ordination.

The units in this structure, however, are on a footing of equality with one another. In Congregationalism each congregation is independent. In Catholic tradition, each diocese, under its bishop, is similarly independent. Unification of the separate units is brought about by some form of "political" government. This government takes shape in endlessly varied political creations—synods, assemblies, general conventions, Church councils. Rome, since 1870, may be an exception since the papacy has replaced even the remnants of conciliar government, though even in the Church of Rome the Pope himself is still subject to "political" election. Rome excepted, however, analogies exist between Catholic and Independent and Presbyterian government. All superimpose, upon congregational or diocesan Church life, government by legislating corporations.

The similarity, however, is balanced by a notable contrast. Catholic Church life gives to organic Church order a far larger control than do the denominational Little Churches. The difference consists in the size of the unit. In Catholic Church life, this is the diocese. The bishop is himself already a unifying *persona ecclesiae*. The independence of the local congregation has already been transcended by way of Church order itself. The bishop is shepherd of an already unified flock. The local minister wields a derivative, not independent, authority. This difference is of momentous importance. History can prove how episcopal Church order (I use the term now in its proper historical sense by which bishop means diocesan Father-in-God) has been an amazingly effective check upon schism. Schisms there have been, to be sure. Eastern Orthodoxy broke with Rome. Anglicanism also broke with Rome, as did the Swedish Lutheran Church. Heretical Church bodies, like the Nestorian Church, carry on in separation in areas once unified under the Church

of the East. But even when schism has occurred, movements
toward unification beckon. Similarity of organic structure
has remained untouched. The Church polities of separated
Catholic Churches may differ radically, yet this need not
prevent intercommunion or ministerial exchange. The
Church of England has a Church polity very different,
indeed, from that of the Episcopal Church in America, yet
both live in one household, the Anglican Communion.

The safeguards against schism in the traditional episcopal
Church order are worth attention. Even apart from constitutional safeguards belonging to Church polity, it is obvious
that the rule requiring three bishops to ordain another bishop
is by itself a great check upon easy sectarian divorces in the
Body of Christ—particularly if bishops remain anchored to
a diocese and are not recognized functionally unless they
have jurisdiction. The diocese is a sizable geographical segment of the whole Church. No bishop can start a new denomination by himself. He must carry at least three bishops
with him, as well as the people of the respective diocesan
jurisdictions. The story of the episcopate in actual fact is,
to be sure, not so simple as this. There have been unattached
bishops in the past, and there are today. The constitutional
safeguards requiring three bishops to ordain and the rule
that a bishop must be actually in living contact with a diocese
have not been adhered to—nor does the Roman doctrine of
orders fully require these checks. Yet episcopal Church
order, despite irregularities, can boast of having maintained
the unity of the historic Church as can no other Church
order. And if it should be anchored once more in a constitutional Church polity which deprived bishops of the power
of irresponsible ordinations, it might be almost unbreakable.
Schism could not well occur except geographically—a whole
nation (as did England at the Reformation) creating a divi-

sion in Christendom. And national churches are very different from denominations.

A full apologia for the historic episcopate is, however, premature. It comes altogether too easily to the mind of an Anglican! My first concern is not the contrast between an episcopal and an independent ministry, but their underlying similarity. The minister in an independent congregation is still functionally a "bishop." He is the *persona ecclesiae* in a smaller segment of the universal Church. If function, indeed, rather than succession, could be thought of as defining the ministry, the problem of Church reunion would be made much easier. The difference between a Catholic Church order and one obtaining in the Free Churches might then no longer be thought of as a complete difference in kind. The difference would rather consist in the size of the unit which offers recognition.

The fundamental structure of Church order is that of table fellowship. Each Holy Supper anywhere in Christendom and throughout the Christian centuries has required a breaker of bread—a functional "bishop." Congregation with "bishop" is a cell of the Body of Christ. It should be, according to New Testament doctrine, the whole Church of Christ manifested in a local assembly. It is conceivable that Catholic Christendom might have developed by maintaining this cellular structure, expressing its catholicity politically, rather than organically, in a Presbyterian or other constitutional form. Instead, Catholic Christianity developed a more complex organic structure—the diocesan episcopate. Most Protestant Churches (Presbyterian Church order partly excepted) have reverted to a more primitive form. In doing so, they lost an organic bond of unity. They substituted the denomination.

If any phenomenon in Church order is a real doctrinal

puzzle, it is the denomination. Just what is it? It isn't "the Church of God which is in Corinth" (1 Cor. 1:2) or "the Church of God which is in Chicago." It isn't a diocese. It symbolizes a doctrinal, not a geographic schism in the Body of Christ. Denominationalism does not mean that the Church in Chicago is out of communion with the Church in Detroit, though that might be tragic enough. It means that one group of Christians in the Church of God in Chicago is out of communion with other Christians in the same Church of God in Chicago. To a denominationally divided Church St. Paul's words could literally apply: "Every one of you saith, I am of Paul and I of Apollos; and I of Cephas; and I of Christ. Is Christ divided?"

Denominationalism may well deserve the judgment voiced by Charles Clayton Morrison in his *What Is Christianity?* when he labels its view of the Church simply heresy and devotes a whole series of chapters to an analysis of the utterly tragic breakdown of corporate Christianity to which this heresy has led—the individualism of Protestant piety, the denial of God in its theory of the origin of a Church in voluntary human association. "The church," so the author describes the congregational theory, "is a voluntary association of individuals, brought into existence *ad hoc* by their association. The church as the catholic body of Christ is an idea only, an abstraction, to which, in thought, a certain mystical veneration may be given, but it has no existence in reality and, on the basis of the strange reading of the New Testament which underlies congregational theory, can have none. The church is, then, not an organic historical community, indwelt by the living Christ who functions savingly through it as his body, but a social contract, and Rousseau should be included among its prophets." "The congregational type of Protestantism tries meticulously to designate the interrelationship of its local churches by nonecclesiastical terms, such as 'associations,' 'Councils,' 'societies,' 'conventions,' and 'brotherhoods' of *churches!* In congregationalism the church exists in the cell, not in the organism." [2]

An Anglican, with episcopal Church order at his back, is tempted to shout his approval of such judgment! Nor is denominationalism likely to find many convinced defenders today in any part of Christendom. A Catholic Church conscience has been reborn in our time. Yet mere indictment of atomistic Protestantism does not itself solve many problems. The Church historian and the theologian can step forward with an incontestable apologia for the Reformation break with Rome and some at least of later schisms within Reformation Christianity. It is an astounding fact, however, that the ecumenical conferences of our generation have been able to disclose sufficient return to unity of faith among Christian communions so that the problem of union has narrowed itself down, for the most part, to one of Church order and sacramental fellowship. Some heresy trials, no doubt, loom ahead. But few Churches today, granted that they share the Reformation heritage, refuse to contemplate reunion on the ground of exclusive possession of basic doctrinal orthodoxy —the ground, be it noted, which led to most sectarian divorces in the first place. We still accuse one another of heresy in ecclesiological doctrine. But this is narrowing the area of conflict enormously.

To return to the debate on this issue. Dr. Morrison is right in accusing denominationalism of losing the New Testament doctrine of the Church as One and Catholic. Yet he

[2] *What Is Christianity?*, Willett, Clark, 1940. Pages 241–242.

makes an important concession. "In congregationalism the church exists in the cell, not in the organism." A cell, too, is still an organic, not an inorganic, structure.

Congregational Church order is a test case, since the more churchly denominations (Presbyterian, Lutheran) already have a structure at least approaching Catholic Church order. The question arises then: Is "the Church existing in the cell" not still the Church? Does it differ in kind from the Church in a more complex corporate form? Does the "breaker of bread" for the cell Church differ in kind from the minister in a congregation under a diocesan bishop? Biological metaphor is inescapable here. Episcopal Church order, let us say, is vertebrate; denominational Church order invertebrate. Granted that this constitutes a very important difference. But, dogmas of succession apart (we shall have to wrestle with these shortly), is this a difference which prevents all mutual recognition? Is it not a difference partly of mere relative organic complexity? Might not a minister in a cell Church receive recognition by an episcopally ordered Church in some way short of reordination? Or, if reordination were pragmatically acceptable, would this mean creating a ministry *de novo?* Does not the Great Church—or better, the "Greater" Church, since the Great Church, too, is in fragments—need the cell Church, as the cell Church, in its turn, needs organic connection with the Church historic and universal? Denominations are more and more recognizing each other's ministries, but is not this recognition one of courtesy? Is not a Church order needed which will give even such interdenominational recognition outward and visible expression? Each denomination still has *organic* unity within its own borders; recognition of a minister is not by courtesy, but by corporate ordination. Is an ecumenical Church achievable except by extension of such organic forms of recognition? And is not episcopal Church order such a form? Its unit is the diocese and not the single congregation. It permits the Church of God in Massachusetts, or Ohio, or California to be a corporate reality—all Christians in communion with one another because all are in table fellowship with a *diocesan* breaker of bread, the bishop. All can, further, be in communion with Christians in other dioceses, since a corporate ordination is necessary for securing the diocesan bishop to begin diocesan Church life at all.

Here I am back to an argument for episcopal Church order once again. Nor do I see how any solution of the problem of Church unity is really possible except under episcopal Church order. Try to imagine the cell Church, with its thousands of units, even when grouped into denominations, achieving unity under some form of Church polity. This is conceivable, perhaps, and Federation has able champions. But Federation does not produce organic unity. The Church of God in Chicago would still not have a corporate table fellowship. Intercommunion might come, to be sure, between denominational Church families. But the families would not yet be one family. Who would preside at a "one family" eucharist? It may seem naïve to hinge the problem of Church unity upon mere geography. Yet geographical fact is involved. If an apostolic epistle were addressed to the "Church of God which is in Chicago," who would receive it? Even in a federated denominationalism, each local cell Church might still have to consult its own denominational headquarters before it could listen or act with corporate approval. The Church of the second and third centuries may have achieved no greater triumph in maintaining the unity of the Church than in creating the diocesan Greater Church, the episcopate symbolizing unity in a geographical area. Diocese and denomination represent two antithetic forms of Church structure. In a diocese one cell Church must live in Christian fellowship with a neighboring cell Church whether it likes such unity or not. Denominationalism permits withdrawal and the substitution of voluntary association across geographical lines. The second is, of course, the more tempting association. But can there be doubt that the first is nearer to the New Testament pattern?

It may seem discourteous to theologians and historians to wrestle with the problem of Church order on purely pragmatic grounds. The more doctrinal considerations will have to be given a hearing also. But pragmatic, contemporary needs may be our best gateway to a unified Church. I feel certain that episcopal Church order, if it finds acceptance at all, will have to commend itself first of all as a practical necessity. And why should not practical need be God's method of leading His people? Defining the contrast between non-episcopal Church order and episcopal Church order in terms of geography and relative size of units is, of course, only part of the story. But it takes the argument between them out of the realm of dogmatic heresy hunting. The people of God, now divided, could recognize one another as still members of a common Body of Christ, within which there had developed differentiations of organic structure.

To unite these differentiated organisms may require delicate ecclesiastical statesmanship. The ministry of the cell Church cannot be equated offhand with the more complex structure of the Greater Church, nor can the two ministries be immediately interchanged. All such problems are, however, capable of solution provided the two Church orders can recognize each other as both true ministries of the people of God. Recognition is the hurdle. The only real divisive force in the Christian family of God is heresy. When community of basic faith in Christ ceases, table fellowship must cease. The Church order of the second century grew up precisely as a protection against heresy. The Reformation break with Catholic Church order was first of all a theological break. Separate and distinct Church orderings were a result, not a cause. The problem of doctrinal unity in the Church is prior to that of table fellowship. The emergence of sectarianism since the Reformation was a witnessing to a deep conviction that the Church was a community of common faith, not a mere legal institution.

But this witness to the importance of doctrine need not be pursued to the point where every article of faith requires a separate community as corporate embodiment. The momentous ecumenical fact of our time is the rediscovery of a community of faith across scores of once sharply drawn denominational boundaries. The old disputes of our forefathers are being dissolved in a new ecumenical brotherhood. A hunger for table fellowship is permeating Reformation Christendom.

And why not mutual recognition, the acceptance of a community of faith? One doctrinal difficulty stands in the way. It is the doctrine, indigenous to Catholic Church order, of Apostolic Succession. Subsidiary to this doctrine is that of the Catholic priesthood. No episcopal Church order, like that retained in Anglicanism, can become a party to any reunion plan unless it has made its peace with this doctrine. Apostolic Succession is, for many who live under episcopal Church order, their most precious possession. Many Anglicans cannot yield this without agony of conscience. Perhaps they cannot yield it at all. Members of non-episcopal churches can little realize how even the suspicion of surrender arouses in large groups of Anglicans a shudder of fear for the safety of the most precious heritage of their faith in the Church of Christ. The subject requires reverent discussion.

The Apostolic Succession

As I launch out on the stormy sea which centuries of controversy have created around the problem of Apostolic Succession, I might be permitted to confess at the outset that I want to see it preserved in the ecumenical Church of the future. I differ from some in my Communion in the doctrinal interpretations which have been attached to it, and which stand in the way of its acceptance by other Reformation Churches.

Ministerial succession, as has been pointed out before, is a fact in all Church life. Every denomination guards a succession today. No cell Church lives utterly to itself alone, either in space or in time. It has a corporate, organic link with other Christian flocks. Succession symbolizes such a link across the barriers which separate passing generations. A vocation is laid upon such a succession. It is charged with preserving purity of doctrine, with maintaining a tradition of custom and moral code. It is the conserving structure within the whirl of change which threatens every social body. Every sect holds precious its organic links with its founding fathers.

Why should such succession be denied the early Church? And why should this succession be denied the descriptive title Apostolic? Here, to be sure, the critical historian may prick a few bubbles. To trace all ministerial successions in the first centuries to one of the original twelve disciples is clearly impossible. Nor is there the slightest evidence that the apostolic college, as such, long perpetuated itself. The emergence of St. James as leader of the Church in Jerusalem at once poses a puzzle. Do we have in Jerusalem an embryonic Caliphate, as appeared later in Mohammedanism? We have no evidence, in the later New Testament period, of three apostles ordaining a new apostle—the rule which later obtains in perpetuating the episcopate. Apostolic power, if St. Paul is a typical apostle, consisted in the ability to institute Church officers by himself.

But give to apostles, or to "apostolic men," the functional definition of missionary founders of the early Churches in the Roman world and the picture comes clear. These are the missionary begetters of Churches—Churches each with local Church officers. The Founder travels to new lands. The local Church must now lead an autonomous life. Replenishment of officers must now take the form of a local succession. This is still the manner in which many a church begins its life on the missionary field today.

And if Apostolic Succession means tracing the successions in Christian history to the Founders of Churches in the apostolic age, who should wish to disprove such historic ministerial genealogy or to belittle the fact that it was held precious and preserved in memory? A Church which could trace its ministerial succession back to an apostolic Founder like St. Peter or St. Paul or St. John would treasure such a tradition and even base upon it assumptions of importance. Succession becomes itself a tradition. A historic ministry takes over the burden of preserving the continuity of the people of God. If this is what is meant by Apostolic Succession, every member of the Church of Christ should rejoice in this link with the divine society born at Pentecost and carried to the ends of the world by the apostles.

A doctrine of an historic ministerial succession traceable

back to the apostolic age is, however, not quite what many Catholics mean by the doctrine of Apostolic Succession. But before defining this doctrine in its Catholic meaning, the story of the rise of episcopacy should be brought on to the scene.

One who boasts of no special competence as Church historian may well tremble as he dares to touch one of the most controversial topics of Christian scholarship. Yet even historians, especially when they give an uncertain verdict, may not be the final arbiters of truth—a truth which cannot be left in an historical vacuum but must be applied to our own pressing problems today. Christian insight and imagination and charity apply also. The story of the rise of the episcopate in the first three centuries is simply not clear. Hence to draw absolute doctrinal conclusions from this story seems impertinent or foolhardy. Historical fact cannot be the only criterion to apply to the Church of our time.

Two theories of the rise of episcopacy mainly hold the field today. One was for long regarded as established by Bishop Lightfoot in his celebrated *Dissertation on the Christian Ministry* (in the Appendix to his commentary on Philippians). According to this, "bishop" and "presbyter" were originally synonymous. Churches were at first governed by colleges of presbyter bishops. Rule by a single bishop emerged out of this earlier more democratic rule. The theory seems to fit many, if not most, of the New Testament allusions to bishops and elders.

A second more recent theory, however, is even simpler and seems to explain the same facts. It has as yet not found as much acceptance as the older theory, but it has many advantages and I give it here at greater length, since it has all along been the foundation of my treatment of the problem in this chapter.[3] This theory sees the rise of episcopacy in the liturgical life of the early Church. The New Testament utilized many ministries of the Spirit, from prophecy to ruling. At the heart of Church life, however, was its central act, the Holy Supper. This required a president, a breaker of bread. In imitation of the Last Supper, this president, representing Christ, was seated at the holy table, with elders, representing the apostles, sitting at his left and his right. Leonardo da Vinci's famous picture of the Last Supper has made this version of an early eucharist familiar throughout the Christian world. The picture corresponds to fact, as Christian art and architecture prove. The typical Christian Church of the early centuries was one in which the holy table was surrounded by seats, all facing the people. The Bishop sat in the center, the elders on each side. Deacons stood, ready to distribute the Communion.

No document in early Church history probably is more frequently cited in connection with the problem of the episcopate than the Letters of St. Ignatius, dating from the early years of the second century. If these are read with the theory of Bishop Lightfoot in mind, they present something of a puzzle. If, however, they are read with the liturgical theory in mind, they give a clear picture. Ignatius pleads for unity in Christian table fellowship. "Wheresoever the bishop shall appear, there let the people be; even as where Jesus may be,

---

[3] The names of such scholars as Sohm and Harnack are sponsors for this theory. It is conveniently and persuasively summarized in Walter Lowrie's *The Church and its Organization*, Longmans, 1904, and the same author's *Problems of Unity*, Longmans, 1924. I once found the reading of these two volumes revolutionary and ultimately satisfying. They have been strangely neglected. Streeter in his fairly recent volume, *The Primitive Church*, takes no account of the Harnack-Sohm-Lowrie theory. The theory is, however, accepted by the Anglican scholar A. E. J. Rawlinson, in an essay in *Foundations*, Macmillan, 1913.

there is the universal Church." [4] "When ye are obedient to the bishop as to Jesus Christ . . . be ye obedient to the presbytery as to the Apostles of Jesus Christ." [5] When Ignatius describes the eucharist "with your revered bishop, and with the fitly wreathed spiritual circlet of your presbytery," [6] he seems to have in mind the circular arrangement of the eucharistic assembly which we can still see in the older basilicas.

This picture of the central act of the early Church also explains the meaning of the subsidiary ministries of presbyters and deacons. The deacons were the table-servers. The presbyters were the "elders" of the parish who naturally were accorded the honor of the chief seats at the holy table. The bishop's position, however, was *unique*. A college of presbyters could not replace him. The presbytery might, indeed, exercise collective advice and rule, with the bishop as chairman. "Shun divisions," says Ignatius, "as the beginning of evils. Do ye all follow your bishop, as Jesus Christ followed the Father, and the presbytery as the Apostles." [7] This early ministerial ordering was congregational—a cell church. A modern Independent Church has some right to boast that it reduplicates this primitive structure. Presbyter and bishop were by no means the same, any more than minister and elders are the same today in a Presbyterian Church. The *name* "bishop" may not always have been used. In the New Testament we meet names such as *appointed elders* (Titus 1:5, 7). A bishop may have been called simply "elder," since he was obviously chosen from among the trusted older men of the parish. His function, not his name,

4 *Ad Smyrn.*, par. 8.
5 *Ad Trall.*, par. 2.
6 *Ad Magn.*, par. 13.
7 *Ad Smyrn.*, par. 8.

was unique, and marked him as the symbol of unity, around whom table fellowship centered. An analogous ambiguity of name, though not of function, still surrounds the words elder, presbyter, and bishop in Presbyterianism today.[8]

Congregational Church life, however, soon faced the problem of subdivision. Assemblies of Christians in a city or region grew too large to preserve table fellowship in a single place. What happened? Ignatius can again furnish a clue. "Let that be held a valid eucharist," he says,[9] "which is under the bishop or one to whom he shall have committed it." A natural deputy would be one of the elders. His serving in the bishop's place, however, was by way of a derivative authority. The bishop's chair remained in each sub-assembly. We know from the account of things in Rome in the third century that when the bishop was absent, a presbyter could not celebrate the eucharist until he had received a particle of the host from the assembly where the bishop himself was present.[10] Much of the story of the development from congregational episcopacy to diocesan episcopacy must be conjecture. The sense of unity of the Church in a single city must have been so strong that diocesan episcopacy arose. The bishop remained the center of unity of the Greater Christian assembly, a fact symbolized in his retention of the power of ordaining presbyters as his deputies. This organic structure proved, as I have argued earlier, to be a marvelously effective device to preserve the unity of the multiplying cell Churches in the spreading and increasingly diversified Christian community.

What has this development, an inquirer may ask, to do

[8] See, on this complicated problem, particularly as concerns the New Testament mingling of the terms "elders" and "bishops," Walter Lowrie, *Problems of Church Unity*, Longmans, 1924, pages 270 ff.

[9] *Ad Smyrn.*, par. 8.

[10] Lowrie, *ibid.*, page 268.

with Apostolic Succession? In one sense, the growth of diocesan episcopacy was most truly a succession from the
Apostles. The bishop was guardian of the apostolic tradition
of Gospel truth. He was the personalized center of the community of faith—a faith going back to the apostolic deposit.
He was a protector of his flock against heresy. "Wherefore,"
says Irenaeus, one of the earliest writers to mention Apostolic Succession, "it is incumbent to obey the presbyters who
are in the Church—those who, as I have shown, possess the
succession from the apostles; those who, together with the
succession of the episcopate, have received the certain gift
of truth (*charisma veritatis certum*), according to the good
pleasure of the Father." [11] This is a common-sense historic
view. The New Testament gradually was accepted as a
deposit of apostolic witness, and became the chief witness
later in Reformation Churches. But in the early Church the
ongoing corporate life of the community was another witness. Only thus could heresy be kept at bay. Every community of believers in later Church history, as a matter of
fact, has trusted a corporate ministerial succession for safe-
guarding its precious store of tradition. And the episcopate
as an organ of continuity and diocesan unity was well fitted
to perform the function of preserving the Church through
the stormy generations of heresy.

It will be noted, however, that the conception of succession we have described thus far is still an historical one. It
was pragmatic and concerned with preserving a tradition of
doctrine as well as table fellowship. The term "historic
episcopate" may well be used to define it. Nor do I see why
it should cause a modern evangelical Protestant any doctrinal qualms. Ministerial succession—episcopal succession,
if you will—could still be defined as a succession of vocation

11 Irenaeus, *Adv. Haer.* 4.26.2.

and of function. It was handed on from bishop to bishop, but only as an authority and a calling given by the Spirit-indwelt corporate body. Validity was not yet thought of as dependent upon a peculiar "grace of orders" monopolized in a succession over the head, as it were, of the Church. In Ignatius or Irenaeus nothing is said of a succession bound up with any special form of ordination or appointment. Instances can be cited of a presbytery ordaining its own bishops (as in Alexandria).[12] The rule requiring three bishops to ordain another bishop was made universal only at the Council of Nicaea. Succession, indeed, is not necessarily tied up with ordination—as the succession in the Roman papacy illustrates.

Just when a view of Apostolic Succession "in the sense of a share in specific Apostolic grace, communicated *ex opere operato*, as through material channels, from one bishop to another, in virtue of certain bodily acts and sacrosanct formulae"[13] became general in the Church, I must leave to historians. It is, in some forms, apparently as ancient as the third century, and has grown in definiteness ever since. It is this doctrine of the Apostolic Succession which constitutes our difficulty today.

The Oxford Movement, launched by Newman and his friends a hundred years ago, was founded upon an uncompromising reassertion of this doctrine. The very first Tract of the series which began the Oxford Movement, and written by Newman, says: "The Lord Jesus Christ gave His Spirit to His Apostles; they, in turn, laid their hands on those who should succeed them; and these again on others; and so the sacred gift has been handed down to our present

[12] Walter Lowrie, *op. cit.*, page 238.
[13] James Vernon Bartlett, *Church Life and Church Order*, Oxford, 1943, page 93.

Bishops, who have appointed us as their assistants, and in some sense representatives."

There, condensed into a single sentence, is the Roman Catholic and Tractarian theory of the ministry. The most important clue to its doctrinal significance is what it says of the Holy Spirit. The Spirit is no longer, as clearly in the New Testament, a corporate possession of the whole Body of Christ, but a gift monopolized by and in a ministerial succession. Episcopate and priesthood (the two go together in a Catholic doctrine of the ministry) are, in rigorist Catholic theory, a channel of divine power unrelated, so it might appear, to the corporate life which they serve. They are independent of it, or at best parallel to it, receiving their power, if succession is added to the picture, from a quasi-legal commission from Christ Himself and maintained in an autonomous sacerdotal caste. Newman's version of the theory does mention the gift of the Holy Spirit. But this only makes the picture more distorted. The Spirit is a corporate possession. How can it be monopolized by a single organ of the Body?

Bishop Frank Weston once argued against the Roman doctrine of the papacy by denouncing its claim that "there is a residuum of Incarnate Activity that requires an isolated form of expression outside the Body proper." [14] Bishop Weston would substitute for the papacy the episcopate and the priesthood generally. But is not the claim still the same? The ministry, as carrier of grace, is independent and autonomous. "Church" is a derivative. Someone has said that for the Roman Catholic hierarchy "Church" as congregation is almost an embarrassment.

Accept this view of the ministry and of succession, and the whole Roman Catholic structure of Church life logically

[14] Frank Weston, *The Fullness of Christ,* Longmans, 1916, page 322.

follows. Sacraments become dependent for their efficacy on the ministry alone. They, too, convey a substantive grace— a grace endangered if the slightest flaw occurs in the genealogy of the sacerdotal succession. Hence the problem of validity leaps to a position of paramount importance. A lapse in technical validity means loss of the life-giving Spirit on which the Church's very existence depends. No valid bishop, no valid priest; no valid priest, no valid eucharist; no valid eucharist, no Body of Christ. Add to the power over the eucharist the power of the keys in the Confessional. This, too, is a power conferrred, not on the corporate Church, but on the sacerdotal order.

It must be admitted that this theory of the ministry can cite at least one text out of the New Testament which looks like incontrovertible authority. It is in the twentieth chapter of the Gospel according to St. John (22, 23). The Disciples after the Resurrection, but before Pentecost, are addressed by Jesus: "Receive ye the Holy Spirit: whose soever sins ye forgive, they are forgiven unto them; whose soever sins ye retain, they are retained." If this is interpreted literally, is accepted as an unquestioned "word of the Lord," and is isolated from the remainder of the New Testament story, as Rome isolates the Petrine text in St. Matthew, the argument, of course, is closed. The Holy Spirit is then a gift monopolized in a sacerdotal succession. The horizontal schism between priesthood and people is complete. Apostolic Succession becomes the *esse* of the Church. Protestant ministries are simply not ministries endowed with priestly powers or the gifts of the Holy Spirit. Protestant sacraments become invalid, including that of Absolution in the Confessional. The Council of Trent is then justified in declaring of the eucharist: "This sacrament no one can effect, unless a priest who has been duly ordained, according to the keys of the Church, which Jesus Christ himself granted to the apostles and their successors." Or again: "Our Lord Jesus Christ, when about to ascend from earth to heaven, left priests His own vicars, as presidents and judges, unto whom all the mortal crimes, into which the faithful of Christ may have fallen, should be carried, in order that, in accordance with the power of the keys, they may pronounce the sentence of forgiveness or retention of sins." [15] The Catechism of the Council of Trent, not illogically, can compare priests to gods: "They represent God on earth. Rightly they are called not merely angels, but gods, since they wield the power and majesty of the eternal God among us." [16]

Here we are at the great watershed of the doctrine of the ministry—as, indeed, of the Church of Christ. I have argued, I trust valiantly, in behalf of the historic episcopate. I shall argue for it again. But unless a view of episcopal Church order can extricate itself from this Roman dogma of a vicarial Apostolic Succession and priesthood, its rejection by evangelical Christendom is foreordained. This theory of the ministry a Biblical Protestantism will never accept. Whether it may remain as a permissive view in an ecumenical Christianity may be a question referred to future ecumenical charity. But a threat of its dominance will wreck any reunion movement in which a Reformation Church is to share. The phrase "historic episcopate" has fortunately replaced "Apostolic Succession" in most ecumenical debate. The suspicion, however, still lingers that the more innocuous phrase is a façade for the other. The Lambeth Conference of 1920, in

[15] Session 14, chapter 5.
[16] Catechism of the Council of Trent 2.7.2, cited in P. T. Forsyth, *Rome, Reunion and Reaction*, Hodder, 1899, page 45: "*Ipsius Dei personam in terris gerunt—quem merito non solum angeli sed dei etiam, quod Dei immortalis vim et numen apud nos teneant, appellantur.*"

its "Appeal to All Christian People," is scrupulous in limiting itself to the words "historic episcopate." The bishops recognize the "spiritual reality of those Communions which do not possess the Episcopate. On the contrary, we thankfully acknowledge that these ministries have been manifestly blessed and owned by the Holy Spirit as effective means of grace." These words may still prove epoch-making. Contrast the reference to the Holy Spirit in this pronouncement with its use in Newman's plea for Apostolic Succession quoted earlier. The Lambeth bishops give the Holy Spirit back to the corporate people of God and include non-episcopal churches in the Body of Christ. At least that is a justifiable inference. Unfortunately a plea for reordination appears in a later paragraph of the "Appeal." Its doctrinal significance is not defined. The vicarial theory of Apostolic Succession, accordingly, *still* lurks in the background. Until this is exorcised, reunion must wait. No evangelical ministry can compromise itself on this fundamental issue.

For this theory of Apostolic Succession denies the Church of God. A schism between priesthood and people is accepted as of the essence of the Church and is read back to the authority of Jesus Himself. Apostolicity has come to mean preservation of this schism. The Johannine text, to be sure, stands as sponsor to this view. The New Testament as a whole is against a sacerdotal interpretation of even this text. Nowhere is priesthood ascribed to an individual. Christ is the only High Priest and the corporate people of God the only priesthood (Heb. 5:7; I Peter 2:5, 9; I John 2:1). That such priesthood can be represented by the ministry should be, of course, accepted. Fear of Roman Catholic error has undoubtedly kept a full expression of the ministry's priestly representation of the Church in check in Protestantism. Remove the fear, and a rich area of rediscovery is disclosed to view.[17] The error, however, is real. P. T. Forsyth describes the Catholic view and the failure of the Catholic Church of history to rectify its root mistake thus: "The priesthood (under the theory of Apostolic Succession) does not flow out of the universal priesthood of the Church conferred by an indwelling Christ, but is parallel with it. Both priesthoods are the gift of Christ, and the one is not representative of the other. Even if Christ appointed the apostles to represent an infant Church which was not yet sufficiently knit or adult to appoint its own representatives, where did He tell them to keep the Church continually in this state of minority? Where did He empower them to monopolize from the Church *in which He dwelt* the continuous appointment of their successors? The theory of an apostolic succession is incompatible with the faith of a Church made priestly by the indwelling Spirit of the great High Priest. Therefore, what the Bishop conveys in ordination is not the priestliness of the Church, but a priestly character conveyed to the episcopate through the apostles over the head of the Church and direct from Christ Himself. And so we read Rome." [18]

Few Anglicans, it must be said in all honesty, would subscribe to an extreme doctrine of Apostolic Succession as Rome (or Newman and some of the Tractarians) formulated it. Liberal Anglo-Catholics (Gore, Moberly, and many others) renounce the view of the ministry as a vicarial priesthood "over the head" of the Church, and anchor it once more in the Body as a representational ministry. The difficulty lingers, however, in that this representational nature of

[17] A remarkable volume describing such possible rediscovery of Catholic emphases in an evangelical ministry is *The Mystery of God* by Wilhelm Stahlin, Student Christian Movement Press, 1937.

[18] P. T. Forsyth, *Rome, Reunion and Reaction.* Hodder, 1899, pages 200 f.

the ministry has not found symbols in a revised view and practice of episcopal succession. Technical solutions of re-union problems are outside my province, but may not a solution come by way of giving the Church not merely constitutional checks upon the episcopate but a place even in episcopal ordinations? Why should not a presbytery share in a rite of laying on of hands as a bishop is consecrated? To admit the representational nature of priesthood is a great gain. But if this is granted only at its source in apostolic times, the succession held to be autonomous since that age, the Roman Catholic error is only disguised. "The representative nature of the priesthood is too remote from the Church's priestly sense at a given time for the Church to feel represented." [19]

A further difficulty looms in the retention by many Anglicans of the theory of an essential difference between a priestly ministry and a prophetic ministry. Protestant ministries, so the argument runs, do not possess a priestly character, make no claim to possess it, and are, accordingly, different in kind from the ministries derived through the Apostolic Succession. Only priestly ministries, it is asserted, can offer sacrifice and possess the power of absolving from sins. The full involvements of this problem would require a separate chapter. Here only a few observations can be ventured.

Priesthood, and the connotations of the word (sacrifice, absolving) are unquestionably emphasized in Catholic traditions as they are not in Protestant traditions. The fear of a sacerdotalism claiming vested rights in the Church's spiritual powers has emptied the ministries in many Protestant Churches of effective use of their own inherent rights. Protestant theologians (P. T. Forsyth is again a conspicuous ex-

[19] P. T. Forsyth, *Ibid.*, page 199.

ample) often confess frankly that Protestant ministries have been impoverished by the loss of the priestly note. If, however, both parties to the dispute could agree that the Christian ministry in any "true" Church is a *representational* ministry, a solution would be in sight. The question then becomes: "Has the Church itself a priestly character and does a particular ministry express this?" Protestant ministries may not be different in kind from "priestly" ministries, but may merely fail in the complete use of an inherent power, as Catholic ministries may neglect, in their turn, equally important functions emphasized in Protestant ministries.

That the Church of Christ is a priestly Body, no Biblical Christianity can deny. New Testament Christianity is priestly or it is nothing. At its center is a priestly cross. Its Lord is the great High Priest Eternal in the heavens. The corporate priesthood of the Church—the priesthood of *all* believers—is of its very essence. Every truly Christian congregation absolves from sins and offers sacrifices of praise and thanksgiving and the memorial of the Lord's death and passion. Every Church, through its ministry, has the power to declare and pronounce to its people being penitent the absolution and remission of their sins. The power of absolving, of taking a sinner back into fellowship, has traditionally been exercised by many an evangelical congregation more conscientiously than in the Confessional of the Roman priesthood. The contrast between the two forms of absolving was that one was corporately exercised, the other vicariously.

And if the Church has this power, a ministry representative of the Church must have it also. The Church's ministry is priestly or it is nothing. Whenever Church and ministry lose their priestly character, the way lies open for tragic losses in the Church's gospel. The Atonement itself may be at stake. Modernist Christianity is in danger of losing the essence of the Christian Faith if it does not recapture this note of priestly offering, of absolving, of sacrifice.

The word "sacrifice" lifts its head here. Clearly, however, the tortured controversies on this subject could see peace also, if the dogma of a vicarial monopoly of grace by a sacerdotal order could once for all be abandoned. The real issue is again whether the Church's offering is vicariously made by a priesthood "over the head" of the Church or is an oblation of the Church as Church. That this is the real issue can be proved from the writings of Luther himself, whose revolt against "the sacrifice of the Mass" has been a cause for Protestant suspicion of the very words sacrifice and priesthood ever since. Luther's violent revolt against the mediaeval view of sacrifice is familiar to all students of Church history. Are his positive words on this matter equally familiar?

"We do not offer Christ as a sacrifice," says Luther, "but Christ offers us. In this way it is permissible, yea, profitable, to call the Mass a sacrifice, not on its own account, but because we offer ourselves as a sacrifice along with Christ; that is, we lay ourselves on Christ by a firm faith in His testament, and appear before God with our prayer, praise, and sacrifice only through Him and through His mediation; and we do not doubt that He is our priest and minister in heaven before God. Such faith, forsooth, brings it to pass that Christ takes up our cause, presents us, our prayer and praise, and also offers Himself for us in heaven. If the Mass were so understood and therefore called a sacrifice, it would be well. Few, however, understand the Mass in this way. For they suppose that only the priest offers the Mass as a sacrifice before God, although this is done and should be done by everyone who receives the sacrament." [20]

This would not be accepted by all Anglicans as a complete description of sacrifice in the Holy Communion, but it goes a long way. The crucial issue, however (and this cannot be emphasized too often), is that it is *monopoly* of priestly powers by an autonomous sacerdotal order, not priesthood as such, against which the Protestant revolt was really directed. A *word* had been poisoned. It needs recovery. The priestly nature of the Church needs recovery. But such recovery does not require submission to a dogma of a difference *in kind* between Protestant and Catholic ministries.

The problem of integrating Reformation ministries with the historic Church order is difficult enough. The decks could be cleared if the view that the two ministries are different *in kind* could be barred from conference chambers. If the Reformation Churches are part of the Church of Christ, they are priestly Churches. Their ministries are priestly ministries. As soon as the ministry is planted in the soil of the corporate life of the people of God, it becomes truly an organ of the Fellowship of the Holy Spirit. Sacraments take on new meaning. The Holy Communion can safely be called a sacrifice. The Real Presence of Christ in the sacrament is then no longer an alien presence brought to earth by a semi-magic formula out of a distant heaven, but a presence of One cradled already in the bosom of the Church. The "grace of orders" becomes the empowering of the servants of the Church with powers inherent in the Fellowship of the Holy Spirit. Succession through a personalized historical transmission becomes a knitting together of fathers and sons in the Faith in Christ. The healing of the

---

[20] Luther, *A Treatise on the New Testament, that is the Holy Mass,* 1520.

schism between the people-Church and the sacerdotal Church would go far toward healing all other schisms in the Church also.

Church and ministry have never been really separated, and should not be. Yet if we wish to understand the Reformation revolt, it must be seen, in part, as a revolt of the Christian people of God against a mistaken view of the ministry. *And the people-Church survived.* It lost organic unity in the revolt. It lost some of its organic links with the Church of history. But the Reformation Churches may have demonstrated that the Holy Spirit cannot be a monopoly of a ministerial caste. The cell Church *can* live and even create ministries—ministries which the historic churches are forced to recognize as at least functionally efficacious, even while they defy the logic of theories of succession or validity. "It is the living body," says William Temple, "which gives authority to its Orders; it is not the possession of valid Orders which gives authority to the body." [21] This truth the Reformation Churches may have proved for all time.

And the Reformation Churches may have recovered for us also the true meaning of the word "apostolic" in the creeds and in any succession theories. The Fourth Book of Calvin's *Institutes* is instructive in this connection. Calvin indulges in no argument against bishops as such. For the episcopal government of the early Church he has nothing but respect. But the doctrine of authority resting merely upon a ministerial succession meets with scorn. Authority lies in true doctrine and doctrine must be apostolic. The teaching of the apostles must ever be the norm for the Church, and the very connotations of the word "apostolic" can pronounce judgment on the corrupt mediaeval system. "In regard to the government of the Church," says Calvin, "nothing can

[21] William Temple, *Church and Nation*, Macmillan, page 195.

be more frivolous than to place the succession in the persons, to the neglect of the doctrine." [22] Seen from the perspective of the centuries of atomized Protestantism, one can easily criticize the Reformers for their blindness in thinking that doctrine would suffice as a substitute for an institutional Church structure. But the Reformers' revolt can be a warning to any succession theory that a mere impeccable genealogical tree is no proof that the ministry is an apostolic ministry. It must be apostolic in function. It must preserve apostolic truth. To rediscover the meaning of the ministry in terms of its function rather than in terms of legal validity may have been one of the blessings which the Protestant era of divided Christendom will bequeath to the ecumenical Church of the future.

The doctrine of Apostolic Succession as a vicarial ministry must go. But does this negative judgment apply to the historic episcopate? Free the argument for the historic episcopate from theories of sacerdotal monopoly. Plant episcopal Church order once more in the evangelical soil of the people-Church. Make it a functional organ of the Body of Christ in time and in space. Can it then make a plea for itself? Anglicanism has received this organic structure of Church life as a heritage from its past. This and its Book of Common Prayer are its most treasured possessions. It feels that it cannot yield these even for the sake of ecumenical peace and unity. Anglicanism has grown humble, however, at least in its wisest moments. The Lambeth "Appeal" makes few arrogant claims. The Anglican plea for the historic episcopate is involved in a paradoxical embarrassment. The episcopate is, in theory, an organ of an ecumenical Church. Yet few of the Anglican Churches in the world are more than minority Churches. In America the Episcopal Church num-

[22] *Institutes*, 4.5.

bers scarcely more than five per cent of the Church popula-
tion in the land. How can Anglicanism win support for the
historic episcopate without exhibiting ecclesiastical snob-
bery? How can it recognize the ministries of the Reformation communions and yet weave them into a more complex
organic structure in which, by the necessity of the structure
itself, they assume a subordinate place as an order of presbyters under bishops—bishops whom Anglicanism already possesses?

I ventured earlier to identify functionally the breaker of
bread in the cell Church with the breaker of bread in the
larger diocesan Church. Both are functional "bishops," and
in the earliest period of Church history were as yet little
differentiated. To superimpose upon the Little Church once
again the more complex order of the Great Church demands
a humbling of prerogative on the part of the ministries of the
Little Churches. In Presbyterian Church polity, the presbyter is already called "bishop in the Church of God." The
historic Episcopal Church order asks him to relinquish this
title! In asking for this sacrifice, the Church order of the
historic episcopate has a great burden of courtesy and Christian charity placed upon it.

I shall not propose concrete solutions. These must be left
to ecumenical statesmanship. If episcopal Church order is to
win ecumenical acceptance, it will have to do at least three
things: First, the purely sacerdotal doctrine of Apostolic
Succession must be surrendered. At the very least, it can
remain only as a permitted theory. Secondly, in some unmistakable way, recognition must be given to nonepiscopal
ministries as true ministries in the Church of God. Thirdly,
the historic episcopate must be defined in ways which will
make it acceptable to evangelical conscience. By way of
pragmatic arguments for it as an organ of unity in the Great

Church, I have probably said enough in earlier paragraphs. A functional order approximating that of a Father-in-God over a presbytery is already emerging in many a denominational Church polity. Episcopal Church order, even though it be at first in denominational, not diocesan, form, is beginning to make its way in ecumenical imagination. But what about the *historic* episcopate?

We are dealing here, I must admit, with a mystery—the mystery of time, the mystery of God, the Lord of time. The Christian flock must be one flock. A bishop as breaker of bread can be the center of unity. It was for this functional and liturgical reason that the episcopate (congregational and then diocesan) arose. But the Christian flock must be one in time also. No Christian Church has ever dared to deny its continuity with the people of God in history. Overtones of meaning still surround the credal words "One," and "Catholic" and "Apostolic" in every Christian confession. And links with the Church of the past exist in many forms. The Catholic, with his emphasis upon Apostolic Succession is in danger of ignoring some of these. The Bible, surely, is one such link—possibly the greatest. The liturgical traditions of the Christian flock are another. Prayers repeated for thousands of years in a communion of saints are a channel of spiritual power that no merely contemporary devoutness can rival. Christian doctrine, witnessed to by generation upon generation, becomes embedded in the very subconscious of the mind of the Church. Can there not be still another such link with the Church of history which is personal —an historical ministry?

The dread word succession meets us here. The historic episcopate is a succession. Though its origins in the apostolic era may be obscure, and its monopoly of apostolic grace denied, it is still there as an historic fact. It may be wellnigh impossible for a Catholic to divorce the historic fact from theories of validity and from genealogical pride. The non-Catholic may see the fact in more neutral perspective. Yet with all reservations, may not a historic personal link with the Church of history have great meaning? Here is a structure of Church life which has lasted from the early centuries. It is the structure of the Church of the East. It is, though overlaid with later growth, the structure of the Church of Rome. It symbolizes, to those who live in it, the Great Church of Christian history. In its Anglican embodiment, it has shared in the reform of the sixteenth century, yet has not broken its organic kinship with mediaeval Christendom. It has an authority of Christian witness given to it by the long centuries of common life in the Body of Christ. Associations have gathered about it as about no other organ of unity. Is it by accident that the word "churchmanship" has found a home in episcopal Church order as it has not elsewhere?

In an address shortly before his death, Dr. William Temple, Archbishop of Canterbury, expressed his appreciation of the historic episcopate and its meaning in Anglican experience. Every Anglican, regardless of doctrinal differences with his fellow churchmen, could echo the Archbishop's words. Of episcopal Church order he said: "In this continuity, we have an effective symbol of that eternity in the midst of time which is the miracle of the Incarnation and the familiar marvel of the Christian Church. Here is something too precious to let go—that chain of laying-on of hands by which, as Bishop Gore rejoiced to say, 'the generations are bound together in one.' In all our aspirations toward Christian unity, this must be held fast." [23]

The problem of an ecumenical ministry is not one of crea-

[23] *The Church Times*, Dec. 17, 1943, page 655.

tion, but of recognition. The ministries are here—in cell Churches, in denominational orderings, in national churches (Sweden is a good example), in great Catholic churches like those of the Orthodox East and of Rome. There is need of an organ which can symbolize unity and continuity and, above all, mutual recognition. Recognition can come by courtesy, as it has already come across many denominational boundaries. But is Catholic conscience wholly wrong when it feels that this is not enough? The reason why it hesitates to accord recognition without some sacramental symbolizing of that recognition is surely not mere arrogance or pride. Even in law a denomination can stand sponsor for organic unity only within its own borders. It may well assert that the cell Church, or gathered communion of cell Churches, is still a fractional part of the Church of God. But a denomination cannot "order" for the universal people of God. The historic episcopate, if accepted by only another fraction of the people of God, as at present, cannot so order either. But, *if accepted*, it could symbolize unity and continuity. It did once, before the age of hierarchical autocracy and its consequent schisms and doctrinal strife. Humbled in its pride, submitting itself once again to apostolic doctrine, and to the corporate Holy Spirit, serving in place of ruling, the historic episcopate may again be the organ which will witness to the world that there exists in time and in space a people of God—one holy catholic and apostolic Church.

INDEX